Inside the
Writer's-Reader's Notebook

A WORKSHOP ESSENTIAL

Linda Rief

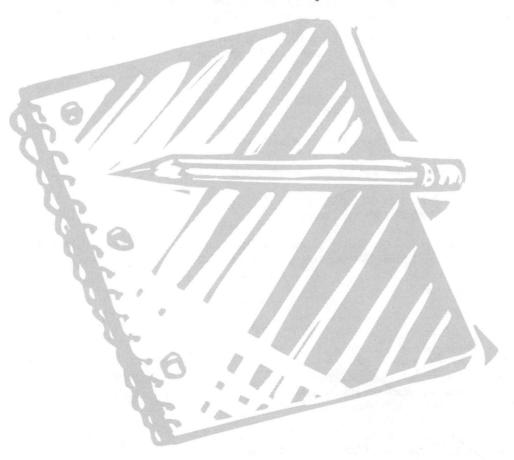

HEINEMANN ❖ PORTSMOUTH, NH

Heinemann
A division of Reed Elsevier Inc.
361 Hanover Street
Portsmouth, NH 03801–3912
www.heinemann.com

Offices and agents throughout the world

The author and publisher wish to thank those who have generously given permission to reprint borrowed material:

"When I Was Young at the Ocean" by Linda Rief and "Crossing the River" by Jesse S. from *100 Quickwrites* by Linda Rief. Copyright © 2003 by Linda Rief. Reprinted by permission of Scholastic Inc.

"Writing-Reading Survey" adapted from *In the Middle* by Nancie Atwell. Copyright © 1998 by Nancie Atwell. Published by Heinemann, Portsmouth, NH. All rights reserved.

Library of Congress Cataloging-in-Publication Data
Rief, Linda.
    Inside the writer's-reader's notebook : a workshop essential / Linda Rief.
       p. cm.
    Includes bibliographical references.
    ISBN-13: 978-0-325-01190-5 (alk. paper)
    ISBN-10: 0-325-01190-7
    1. English language—Composition and exercises—Study and teaching (Elementary)—United States.
  2. Creative writing (Elementary education)—United States. I. Title.
    LB1576.R5193 2007
    372.62'3—dc22   2007021394

Editor: Lisa Luedeke
Production: Patricia Adams
Typesetter: Tom Allen/Pear Graphic Design
Cover and interior design: Jenny Jensen Greenleaf
Manufacturing: Louise Richardson

Printed in the United States of America on acid-free paper

11 10 09 08 07 VP 1 2 3 4 5

~For Donald M. Murray~
Inspired by his daybook, I began my own in 1986.
I've been keeping one ever since.

AND

~For Maureen Barbieri~
"It is not often that someone comes along
Who is a true friend and a good writer.
[Maureen] is both."
E. B. White, *Charlotte's Web*

Contents

Acknowledgments

T hank you to the several thousand students I have had in nearly twenty-five years of teaching, who have taught me how the *Writer's-Reader's Notebook* works best for each of them. Their thinking, through their reading, writing, and drawing, has taught me how to refine my teaching and broaden my learning. Their willingness to share that thinking allows and encourages other students to deepen their own thinking. Their notes over the years have reinforced for me how these notebooks have continued to be central in their life-long pursuit of learning.

Don Murray reinforced the habit of keeping a notebook for me each time he opened his daybook through his writing or speaking. Ralph Fletcher's books about writers' notebooks continue to help me guide my students through theirs. Karen Ernst showed me how to extend my thinking through sketching. Maureen Barbieri and I have taken our notebooks with us—to islands off the coast of Maine and New Hampshire, to coffee shops, gardens and museums—on the rare occasions when we take a day or two just to talk, write, and draw. Tom Romano's and Nancie Atwell's teaching, learning, writing, and research continue to ground and frame all that I do as an educator and learner myself. You have all been central to how these notebooks have evolved and how valuable they are to me as a teacher and person, and to my students. Thank you.

So many teachers in courses I have taught for the University of New Hampshire and Northeastern University, and in workshops all over the United States, in Canada, and in Europe have added to my thinking about notebooks through their questions and through their willingness to take risks through their writing and drawing. Thank you for all you do as learners to help so many kids become the most articulate, literate young men and women they can be.

To the skilled, passionate, dedicated Heinemann folks, who take their desire to provide the strongest, most beneficial professional resources to educators so seriously, thank you for working so hard on each aspect of this project: Lisa Luedeke, editor; Patty Adams, production editor, Abigail Heim, production supervisor; Jenny Jensen Greenleaf, cover and interior designer; Louise Richardson, manufacturing; Stephanie Colado, editorial coordinator; Erik Chalek, marketing copywriter; and Olivia Reed, permissions assistant.

Introduction

When I was twelve, I read <u>Anne Frank: The Diary of a Young Girl</u>. Every year I re-read it, along with more current books and documentaries. The true beauty of Anne Frank's diary is that she always sounds so incredibly real. Her diary makes the Holocaust personal, not political; individual, not anonymous.

I wrote Julie Weiss's diary with Anne Frank's near me at all times so I wouldn't forget, truly, what I was doing. It was a constant source of inspiration. (Denenberg 2000)

This may be the best idea anyone could give us as teachers, especially teachers of writing—to keep Anne Frank's diary near us at all times so that we make sure all we ask our students to do is *personal, individual,* and *real.* This means keeping kids central to all we do, and keeping real writing and real reading at the heart of the language arts. It means knowing our kids well enough that we can build on their strengths and promises. It means teaching with our head and our heart because kids learn better when we know them, respect them, and care about them.

For me, this means designing my classroom as a writers-readers workshop, where we are doing personal, individualized, and real writing and reading. I believe our kids can do their best work as writers and readers in a workshop approach when given

- ◆ time

- ◆ choice

- ◆ response
  This is what you did well.
  These are the questions you need to consider.
  Try this suggestion or two.

- ◆ models of fine writing and reading, both fiction and nonfiction, that engage, interest, and challenge

In designing my classroom as a writers-readers workshop, I give students *choices* and *time*: choices about what they write and read, time to develop their ideas as writers, and time to read books of their choice. I also provide constructive written and oral feedback to their drafts of writing and their reading in progress, as well as good models of both from which to learn.

I want the writing they do to be for real reasons for a real audience, not a meaningless exercise meant only for the teacher. I want them to write because they have something to say or to figure out. I expect students to draft and redraft their writing based on conferences with me and their peers. I expect them to do a lot of writing in order to discover their strongest, most meaningful writing. I expect them to read for the pleasure of a good book—because they wonder what someone else has to say or is trying to figure out. By the time kids leave my classroom, I hope they have grown as writers and readers, that they recognize that growth and have gained enough skills and confidence to face any reading or writing task, and that they like writing and reading enough to embrace them for life.

PART I

How to Use the Writer's-Reader's Notebook

The *Writer's-Reader's Notebook*

The *Writer's-Reader's Notebook* (*W-RN*) has been crucial to the work my students and I do as writers and readers. It gives students a place to be personal, individual, and real as they take notice of themselves and their world. It is their thinking for their own reasons, and it is the best tool I have ever used that allows students to develop their voices.

The *W-RN* is at the core of all I expect from adolescents because it allows them *choice*, *time*, and *practice* with regard to writing and reading. It gives me a place to learn about each of them personally and individually. It shows me who they are—their strengths, their promises, their questions, their weaknesses—so I know how to push and challenge them. It shows me what I am teaching well and what I still need to teach. Even in a classroom filled with twenty-five or more students, this is the most important tool I have that allows me to teach to the individual while teaching to the class.

The *W-RN* supports my goals as a teacher, giving students a place to begin and develop their ideas as writers and readers and giving me a place to see their growth. It supports my belief that kids grow as writers and readers when they have the opportunities to do a lot of

writing and reading. The *W-RN* gets them in the habit of observing and thinking about all they notice. It supports my belief that kids' voices need to be heard as they wonder, question, argue, reason, change their minds, or affirm their thinking.

The *W-RN* provides a structure that gives consistency in form and function for the students as learners and for me as a teacher; it allows, encourages, invites, and teaches kids to be themselves in the pages. The structure enables them to be more productive and more thoughtful.

As students use their *W-RNs*, they learn to recognize their development as more thoughtful, more critical, more fluent, more creative, more imaginative writers and readers. Through the notes I write to them, their notebooks provide the place where I can nudge, challenge, encourage, verify, question, and push students' thinking.

How *This* Writing-Reading Notebook Evolved

I have discovered that giving students a blank notebook and total freedom overwhelms many kids. A handful of students I have each year arrive on the first day of school with their own notebooks—ones they have chosen for the size and feel, and ones they have been keeping on their own for several years. These students know exactly what to do. They have already made the notebooks their own. They have heard from former students that they will need to keep a journal (notebook), and they are thrilled. Not so for many other students.

The majority of the hundred-plus students I have each year arrive with only questions: How big does the notebook have to be? How many pages does it have to have? Should it have lined or unlined paper? Loose-leaf paper or spiral bound? How soon do we need it? What do you want us to write in it?

For several years I tried to have the students buy and bring their own notebooks to class. I tried to get them to understand what Jean Little says about journals in her book *Hey World, Here I Am!*: "Getting a journal is like buying shoes. You have to find the one that fits. And you are the only person who can tell if it pinches" (1986, 74).

"The one that feels best in your hands. The size you want. The kind of paper you want. And try to have one by the end of this week so we can begin writing right away," I said.

Weeks after school started, fewer than half had a notebook. I was handing single sheets of paper to students, saying, "Add this to your notebook as soon as you get it. Tomorrow, maybe?" The single sheets of paper disappeared.

And their questions were endless: What color should we get? Should it be divided into sections? Can I use the notebook I use for all the other classes? Is this too big? Is this too small? They needed more guidelines, more structure.

Experiment failed: buying their own didn't work—for most students, that is. I ended up either buying notebooks for all of these students or begging the secretary to find me some composition books despite the fact I hadn't ordered any the year before.

I thought, *All right, there must be a better way.* I began searching for notebooks that I could buy for them. I'd have students reimburse me at the beginning of the year. Each year I found a different bargain and bought a hundred-plus notebooks. Each year I thought I had found the perfect writing-reading notebook, and each year I found out why these notebooks were such a bargain. The paper was too thin, so students could write only on one side. Or the paper ripped out of the binding too easily. Or the binding fell apart and whole chunks of paper disappeared. Or the covers weren't heavy enough to last the year. Or the covers were too "girlish" or too "boyish."

One year I bought all the materials so the kids could design and decoupage their own covers. It took days to instruct them and complete the covers. I had one hundred notebooks spread all over windowsills, bookcases, and tables for *weeks* drying. They never dried completely, often sticking to each other when they were handed in.

The *inside* of the notebooks was another story. I will spare you the year-after-year grisly details, but imagine the scene: scissors, glue sticks, tape, rulers, staplers—and twenty-three to twenty-eight eighth graders per class. And twelve- to fifteen-page packets for each student. These were the lists and expectations for each section of the notebook that I was going to have the kids insert into their blank books. They were my notes to the students that had evolved over my years of answering questions and noticing what worked best to allow them to write and to read.

Surrounded by bits of paper floating to the floor, I watched kids glue the wrong pages to the wrong sections with mountainous lumps of glue (despite verbal, written, and drawn instructions!), search for staple removers, and compete for scissors, rulers, and tape. Stepping back from this scene, I heard myself saying, out loud, and to no one in particular, "I wish I could get someone to print a notebook that was sectioned and organized and had everything already printed in it."

Aha! Was that a possibility? Would a publisher believe that this would be a valuable tool for students and other teachers in other classrooms also? One did. And this guide and the *Writer's-Reader's Notebook* are the result.

The *W-RN* has evolved over a long period of time and through much trial and error. The way the notebook looks and feels today, the sections it contains, how it is organized, the kinds of lists I have included, my expectations and goals written right in it, even the number of pages per section and the quotations from writers and students grew out of my continual attempts to create a space where very specific kinds of learning could happen for my students.

You have the intentional choices my students and I made for the *W-RN* in front of you. It includes a heavy cover that will endure the abuse of overstuffed lockers and teenagers' bedrooms. It's a cover that appeals to kids yet one that they can personalize. A strong, flexible spiral binding that allows kids to completely turn the pages without them ripping out. A heavy bond paper that will allow students to write and draw smoothly and on both sides. All my expectations and instructions are printed in the appropriate sections on cardstock that won't tear out—they don't have to be glued in. These expectations have evolved over time to allow kids many choices.

I was excited to think we could actually get the notebook printed in the format the students and I worked for years to develop.

But wait . . . an "Oh, no!" moment.

November. I am at the National Council of Teachers of English annual conference. I am

sitting in the audience of a session on writer's notebooks, listening to a person I deeply respect for his writing and knowledge of notebooks. He says, "I would no more tell kids how to organize their notebooks than I would how to organize their wallets."

Oh, no! I think. *I will never get this right with kids. Professional colleagues like this presenter will think I'm a teaching failure because I am telling kids how to organize their notebooks.* I leave the session feeling terrible, believing I will have to tell the publisher that I can't do this, it's a bad idea.

But wait. Think this out, Linda. You have tried everything over the past twenty years—no structure, no requirements, no expectations, a blank notebook, as well as different structures, organizational patterns, and varied expectations. The blank notebooks with no guidelines, no structure, no expectations worked for only a few kids. Very few.

I had to bring to bear my own experience. I had to listen to what I had learned from my own students. The notebook I'd created over time was the structure (or the design) that had worked for the *most* kids—and it was students' suggestions that guided the notebook's development.

My students are not professional writers with the well-established habit of writing daily in a notebook. They don't know the benefits. They have to try it. And maybe they have to try it in a more systematic way in order to find the way that works best for them. Only then will keeping a notebook become a habit.

What I had discovered in my own classroom was this: giving kids an organizational frame in which to write, along with specific expectations, gave students the *freedom* to write.

I like to think about that wallet a little differently—there are sections for bills, sections for credit cards, a section for a license. It is not a wad of leather with a wide, empty, cavernous space waiting to be filled. It is shaped and organized with *intent*; designers know what the person using it will find most helpful. The designer has the user in mind and bases the design on suggestions, previous experience, and knowledge gleaned from using a wallet herself. The wallet keeper then fills it with what he wants in there, what he finds most useful in each space that has been provided with his individual needs in mind.

That is what I have been doing with the notebooks. I've tried all kinds of designs and have paid close attention to what organizational frames, what size, what materials, and what expectations best help kids "fill their wallets" so they can focus their attention on what they need and want to say.

Outside of my own classroom many teachers attending presentations and workshops I conduct have asked me to provide the details of how these notebooks are structured, in both format and expectations. I am confident that what works for my kids will work for many other kids and many other teachers. I hope what I have found with my students will be helpful for you and your students.

Keeping a Reading-Writing Notebook

For many students, this will be the first time they've been asked to keep a writing-reading notebook. The task seems daunting, even when I explain to kids that what goes into the notebook *is* wide open. And that may be why keeping a notebook is so perplexing—it is wide open, even with the structure I provide. "Show me who you are as you think about yourself, about books and reading, about the world around you. What do you notice all around you?" I say. I explain that they could use the notebook to

- gather ideas for writing
- record, respond, and react to nightly reading by writing or drawing
- hold on to memories (whether they feel significant or relevant, insignificant or irrelevant at the moment)

- record thoughts, observations, and questions about their immediate world or the world at large
- question reading, writing, learning
- take out frustration, fear, anger, or sadness
- remember everything that makes them happiest
- work out who they are by thinking about all that matters or doesn't matter to them
- keep ideas in one place so they don't lose their thinking
- establish the habits of collecting, noticing, listening, and writing
- practice writing

Ultimately, the purpose of the *W-RN* for us as teachers is to see that our students are learning, changing, and deepening their thinking and insights. This is our evidence, and theirs, of growth over time.

The Shape, Materials, and Organization of the *Writer's-Reader's Notebook*

The Size, Cover, and Materials

Over the years I've found that an organizational structure gives students a sense of security and comfort so they can write more freely and honestly. And, I admit, the consistency in size and structure of the sections of the notebook helps me when reading and responding to more than a hundred notebooks every two weeks.

The students prefer a smaller size, not the 8½-by-11-inch size of most notebooks they are asked to use in school. The smaller size fits nicely in their hands or laps as they are reading paperbacks, and it feels more like a journal, a personal space for thinking. The size of each page is less ominous—it's a size students believe they can fill because it is not overwhelmingly large. Instructions and lists are printed on cardstock to give more permanence, so they won't fall out and disappear. The cardstock also enables kids to easily locate and return to a page again and again as they add titles and ideas to these lists.

Most students also prefer lightly lined paper. Although I would rather leave the pages blank to invite drawing, the lines make it easier for kids to write. I keep a pile of heavier white art paper, cut just a bit smaller than the notebook pages, so kids have thicker paper on which to draw. They can easily glue it into the notebook. This way they choose where and when to insert a drawing.

The cover, made of a strong, heavy paper so that it survives a year, has been left blank. Suggest to kids that they personalize the notebooks by designing their own cover. They could do this in many ways; here are just a few ideas:

- Students can make a collage—use the front cover for pictures or words of things they like to do, places they love to go.

- Read "My Name" from *The House on Mango Street* (Cisneros 1989) to the students. Have them do a quickwrite in response to this vignette (in the "Response" section of the *W-RN*). Ask, "What does this bring to mind about your name?" Have kids research their names: What do you know about your name? Where did it come from? What does it mean? How well does it fit? Have you ever wanted to change it? To what? Why? Have them put their name and the history and meaning of their name in words and drawings on the front cover.

- Have them draw their first name in pictures showing what they like or do. See sketch in the appendix on page 178.
- Students can make a Heart Map, as described in Georgia Heard's *Awakening the Heart* (1999).

Show them all the possibilities for personalizing their notebooks or leaving them as they are, and give them a choice about what makes the most sense for each one of them. The covers of the notebooks don't have to be the same. Covering any pictures or drawings they choose to add with clear contact paper or a coat of gesso, a sealant found in any craft store, will preserve the cover and help it last in backpacks and lockers.

Organizational Structure of the Notebook

The *W-RN* is organized into the following sections:

Front Matter
> *Introduction and Expectations*
> *Books I Am Currently Reading*
> *Books I Want to Read*
> *Ideas for Writing*

Response

Notes

Vocabulary

Spelling Matters

Introduction and Expectations

The two-page introduction and synopsis of expectations evolved over time as students showed me what they were capable of and what pushed them beyond their comfort zones. They want these expectations right up front—this is what is *expected of me as I use this W-RN*. Having these instructions printed in the notebook helps students (and parents) know what to do. It is a constant reminder of the notebook's ongoing use. Because it's printed right in the book, it can't be lost in the black hole of some adolescent lockers.

I purposely left several pieces of the expectations blank. You have to decide with your students how often, and for how long, you expect them to read during a week. You also have to decide how many pages they are capable of filling in a week's time. It is not the same for all students. It is a matter of figuring out the strengths of each student and deciding what amount of work makes sense to keep each one growing as a reader and a writer, without pushing beyond his or her reach. It's also a matter of how you want them to best use the

W-RN. What class is it for? What are the goals? What do you want your students to know and be able to do by the time they leave your classroom? How can this notebook help meet those goals?

Books I Am Currently Reading

I developed the reading list because I wanted students to see just how much they were actually reading, or not reading. When I started keeping my own list, I was amazed at how many books I actually read. I want kids to see this also.

Students list the title of the book they are currently reading and the date they begin reading, only once, when they begin the book. These are books they choose on their own. I expect students at the eighth-grade level to read for a half hour five nights per week. I don't think that is too much to ask, and I think it's necessary to establish and preserve the habit of daily reading.

Asking kids to maintain a list of books they are currently reading is helpful in so many ways. From the information they give me on this list, I can tell

- what kinds of books, topics, and authors they like and don't like
- which books I can recommend to them to enhance or vary their selections
- which books I might put in their hands to help them read faster, or more slowly, or to read at all
- whether to suggest they abandon a choice (because it seems to be taking too long to read) and try something else
- who these kids are as readers or nonreaders
- whether they are growing or changing as readers
- how long it takes them to read books
- if and how they read deeply (same genre or author) and widely (range of authors or genres)
- books they might recommend to others based on their personal appeal

Why don't I have them read daily in class? My class periods are only forty-five to fifty minutes long, five days per week. I have to decide what I can do in that time and what is best done at home. You need to decide how much time you can expect your students to read at night, and how often during the week, and have them fill in the blanks once you decide.

Every Friday we do read silently in class for a half hour. This gives me the chance to see if kids are really committed to the books they have chosen and to put other books in their hands if they are not. Once everyone has a book and is reading, I read for at least ten minutes to establish the silence we all need to read well.

This is the only time during the week, however, when I can then move quickly from student to student, clipboard and chart in hand, noting what book and page each is on and how much each has progressed since the previous week. Nancie Atwell (2007) does this daily in order to keep a solid record of her kids' reading. She has the time; I do not. Asking the kids once a week to show me what page they are on is the best I can do under the constraints of my schedule and the number of students I teach.

If the students are not moving forward in their reading, I can try to figure out why: they need a more compelling book, they are not taking my homework seriously, or they have had a number of other major commitments during the week that pushed their reading to the bottom of the pile. We can then work to solve the problem together.

There is still time on Fridays for one of the following:

◆ *Read-arounds*: I've found that there are times I can put out a number of books connected in some way (new authors, genre, theme, etc.) and introduce them to students by having the kids read the first three pages of each book instead of listening to a book talk. I often do this for books that I don't know well enough to talk about but know other kids or teachers or professional reviews have recommended.

   I put a stack of seven to ten books on each table where kids sit. This stack might be focused on young adult (YA) authors, or fantasy, or poetry, or the Holocaust, or graphic novels, and so on. Students must read the first three pages of at least five of these books. If they find one they really like, they check it out. If they find more than one, they add the books to their "Books I Want to Read" list so they will remember them. I tell them to note the cover, read the inside or back cover, and pay attention to the tone, the choice of words, the topic, and the lead. What is it that pulls them in, makes them want to read this book?

◆ *Short book talks*, by me, by students, or by the librarians, to introduce books or authors. I like to read the lead or a short passage, so the kids hear the tone and voice of the author, while giving a short synopsis of the story and what it was that kept me reading it. I make sure the kids have their "Books I Want to Read" list open in front of them so they can note the titles that seem appealing to them.

   After I model book talks, perhaps more appropriately called *book chats* for their informality, I ask students to share their favorite books. We put these favorite books or highly recommended books up on the wall on easy-to-read lists:

   books recommended by the previous year's students

   books and authors my current students or I recommend

   new books and authors introduced by the librarians, others, or through compelling reviews

Since our silent reading day is Friday, it makes s,ense to have these book talks at the beginning of each period on those days. A schedule might look like this:

first Friday of the month: teacher book talks

second Friday of the month: student book talks

third Friday of the month: librarian book talks

fourth Friday of the month: Read-arounds (see above)

◆ *Minilessons connected to the process of reading* (students record these in their "Notes" section):

how to find books in the classroom library

how to check out and return books

how to figure out whether you want to keep reading or abandon a book

how to use the W-RN *while reading*

expectations during silent reading time

how to give a book talk

differences between reading for pleasure and reading for information and the strategies that are more helpful for each

how to skim or scan and reasons for each

how to make notations in the book to relocate vocabulary, passages, or what you were thinking as you read, without losing the "reading zone" (Atwell 2007)

how to write or draw what you were thinking as you read (Students write or draw in the "Response" section.)

how to share a finding about a vocabulary word

Sometimes I give students a short passage written by an author (preferably connected to one of the books recommended that day or previously) in which the author talks about his or her reading process. I either place the passage on the overhead or ask the kids to glue it into their "Response" section, and ask students to respond or react to what that author said.

Doing *one* of these activities in conjunction with silent reading one day of the week is about all that can be accomplished, unless you have more than fifty minutes in a class period.

When I read the students' notebooks weekly, I put the date next to the last book on their list, so I can begin to tell how many books they are reading, or not reading during a specific length of time, usually two weeks. Based on what I notice on this list, I can add that information to the note I write to each student in the "Response" section. (See Chapter 6 and Student Samples in Part II for details on how I respond to and evaluate these notebooks.)

Books I Want to Read

The "Books I Want to Read" list came to be because we—both students and I—often forgot the title of a recommended book because we either didn't write it down or couldn't find where we had written it down. This gives us a specific place to record these titles.

I remind kids to turn to this section when we have book talks, usually on Fridays. If I or a student mentions a book that sounds interesting, I tell the kids to add it to their list. Noting who recommended the book and what made it seem interesting enough to want to pick it up provides enough of a reminder to make the effort to find the book. The books on this list can also come from

- the list of highly recommended books we compile from previous and current students, which I put on the wall at the beginning of the year and we add to throughout the year (Your list will look different, which is why we each have to compile our own from our particular students.)

- the Book Review Binder, which is filled with book reviews from previous and current students and the students of Syd Korsunsky in Winnipeg, Canada, who showed me what his students were doing and how to keep this three-ring binder (As your students write book reviews, add them to your binder for other kids to read.)

- books they see friends reading or that have been recommended to them

- quick one- to two-minute book recommendations that students give on Fridays after we read silently for at least half an hour

- professional reviews by writers or other students published in newspapers and journals, such as *The New York Times Book Review* and *Voices from the Middle.* (Add the ones you read to your Book Review Binder.)

Ideas for Writing

Keeping a separate list of ideas for writing is also a good idea, as it gives kids a convenient, easy-to-locate, accessible list of possible topics for writing. Noting how they came up with the idea also gives them deeper memories about what they were thinking at the time and, therefore, a stronger commitment to getting back to that idea. Remind students that as they read books, as they hear the stories of others when they share and confer about their writing, as they go places and do things with friends and family, as they listen to the news, and so on, ideas may pop into their heads, and they should add them to the "Ideas for Writing" list for future reference.

Every few weeks, ask kids to go back through their notebook and find places that give them writing ideas. Have them jot those down on this list, perhaps even referencing the page number from their "Response" section, where they first mentioned this idea.

Response

In the "Response" section, students explore ideas for writing, write or draw reactions to books they read for nightly homework, do their quickwrites in response to short pieces of writing I read to them at the beginning of class, and note their observations of themselves, others, and the world. For the majority of students, I expect anywhere from one to three pages of response per week. Response can be written, drawn, or collected (poems, photographs, pictures, cartoons, lists, quotations, excerpts, statistics, song lyrics, editorials, and so on). When students glue something in this section, I expect them to tell me why they put it there and what it means to them.

Note on the page that introduces this section that I have left blank the number of pages students are required to produce each week. You have to negotiate this with students as a whole, and with some students individually. Students with special needs may require a different goal based on what they believe they are capable of and what you believe will help nudge them forward. We want all our kids to grow, so we must consider where they are as readers and writers when they come to us and what we can do to push and challenge them to get better.

Most of this writing is done at home at night. However, several times a week I put short pieces of writing on the overhead projector, asking kids to either write anything the piece brings to mind or to borrow a line and let the line lead their thinking. I have them write as fast as they can for two minutes (see Rief 2003). These short pieces—poetry, op-eds, reviews, essays, excerpts from novels—are *always connected* to what our focus is for the quarter (see the Appendix for two sample quickwrite activities). In the "References and Recommended Resources" section of this guide, I have listed other books I use that get kids started writing and that can also be used for quickwrites.

I give kids a variety of options and choices regarding how they use the pages in the "Response" section. The Appendix contains a set of notes I refer to when talking to kids about how to use this section (see "Notes for the Teacher to Guide Students' Notebook Response"). I used to give a copy of these notes to the kids to tape into their notebooks, but I found they didn't read them or really listen to them if I read them aloud. It is more helpful to use this page as a guide for myself as I talk to the students about the kind of writing they might do in their *W-RNs*, and show them examples from previous students.

In Part II of this guide you will find handwritten or typed pages taken directly from my students' and my own *W-RNs*. I make transparencies of pages from former students, read each to my current students as they look at it on the overhead, and ask them to jot down what they notice the writers are doing in their notebooks. These examples from former students help my current students the most. We make a list of ideas generated by these examples on the overhead.

If your students have never kept *W-RNs*, or you have no examples from previous students, use the examples from my kids—make transparencies of the samples in Part II.

Ask your students: "What do you notice these kids are doing in their notebooks?" Collect their responses on the overhead and have them write down this list in the "Notes" section. Title the list "Possible Ways to Use the Notebook," and have your kids write this title on the table of contents at the front of the "Notes" section. This will also show students how to use the "Notes" section and the table of contents.

Start collecting your own examples from your students—the things they do that surprise, amaze, gratify, perplex, inform, sadden, thrill, and teach you. The things that show their thinking, their playing. Ask them if you could make a copy and share their thinking with other students. Put these pages on the overhead and talk about what makes each example an effective way to use the notebook. Invite your students to talk about what they notice they do and how that is helpful to them as a reader or writer.

Getting the Kids Started

In Chapter 7 of *Lasting Impressions*, Shelley Harwayne (1992) writes about how to use literature to introduce students to how they might use *W-RNs*. Her book is a terrific source of ideas for ways to get kids thinking about all they have to say. In my classroom, I read poetry, picture books, and excerpts from memoirs that help students connect to their own memories of past and present experiences and then ask kids to do quickwrites (Rief 2003) in response to these short pieces. These short read-alouds have been the most helpful in convincing kids that they *do* have things to say. My book *100 Quickwrites* is organized around my curriculum plan for the year, so the beginning of the book is filled with many of the poems and short pieces I use to get the kids thinking about themselves. I have listed several other books in this guide's "References and Recommended Resources" section that also help kids begin, and continue, to write. (See the Appendix for two quick-write activities.)

You will find the "Response" section of the *W-RN* is filled with short quotes from authors, poets, and students about their use of journals or notebooks. From time to time, you might point these out to your students and ask them to jot down anything these passages remind them of in their own experience as writers or readers or artists. Do they agree or disagree with what is said? What does a particular quote bring to mind for them?

The Bookmark

I also give the kids a bookmark I make that helps nudge them to explore their thinking as they read, write, and notice things in the world (see Appendix). I make a copy of this bookmark for each student on cardstock, put their name on it, and have them personalize the bookmark by writing their favorite quotes—usually focused on reading or writing—on the back. I then laminate the bookmarks and give them back, suggesting the students use them as they read and write, especially if they are stuck for ideas.

As I read a short piece to the students, perhaps a short story or poem, editorial or essay, I have them use the bookmark starters to respond to that reading as a model for the way they might use it on their own.

Poetry Find

The first few days of school I also do a Poetry Find. I collect poems that I know will speak to my kids, written by poets I admire on subjects that have to do with writing or reading or adolescents. I type the poems and then cut them into enough pieces so that I have one piece for each student in the class. (With four classes, this means I have four sets of poems cut into the appropriate number of stanzas depending on the number of kids in each class.) I put the various pieces (four or more lines each) of the poems into one basket, all mixed up, hand the basket around, and have each of the kids choose one piece.

They must read their stanza to themselves and then walk around the room, finding the other students holding the remaining pieces of their poem. I mention that they should think about the subject, the tone, the speaker, and the format to help them find other stanzas that seem to match. (All poems should be in the same font, same type size, and on the same color paper so they can't be matched through appearance.) All those students who think they belong together must sit together, read the stanzas aloud, and determine the most sensible order. They figure out the meaning and the pronunciation of unknown words (from the dictionary, a peer, or me).

Once every table of students has finished organizing their poem and practiced reading it with voice and spark, I have them read the poem aloud to the whole class. (Sometimes they are *not* in the exact order in which the poet wrote them, but if the order makes sense, that's okay.) We hear all of them. We talk about each one. What did you notice about the poem? What did you like? What surprised you? What confused you? What do you think this is about? What lines make you think that?

I talk about what I know about these poets and why I chose these poems. I then ask the students to each choose the one poem they like most (I have copies of the whole poems already printed up) and glue it into the "Response" section of their notebook. I give them two to three minutes to then respond to the poem: What made you choose this one? What did you like most about it? What does the poem bring to mind for you?

Following are some of the poems I use for this activity:

"The Writer," by Richard Wilbur (1988)

"Owl Pellets," by Ralph Fletcher (1998)

"Hockey," by Scott Blaine (Knudson and Swenson 1988)

"The Sidewalk Racer," by Lillian Morrison (Knudson and Swenson 1988)

"Swinging the River," by Charles Harper Webb (Janeczko 1991)

"The Summer Day," by Mary Oliver (1992)

"Traveling Through the Dark," by William Stafford (1998)

"Daydreamers," by Eloise Greenfield (1981)

"Bully Lessons" and "Always Take a Dog," by Joyce Sidman (2003)

"Boyz n Search of Their Soular System," by Eugene Redmond (Feelings 1993)

"I Love the Look of Words," by Maya Angelou (Feelings 1993)

"This Is Just to Say," by William Carlos Williams (MacGowan 2004)

"The Road Not Taken," by Robert Frost (Schmidt 1994)

"On Turning Ten," "First Reader," and "Introduction to Poetry," by Billy Collins (2001)

Although I do the Poetry Find only at the beginning of the year, I do ask students to find and respond to one poem a month that is significant to them personally. I want to open students' minds and hearts to poetry. Even though I have more than a hundred anthologies of poetry from which they can select a poem of their own choice to copy and respond to, I think it is helpful for me to open these collections to them by frequently reading a variety of kinds of poetry aloud and talking about the various poets. I even give kids a list of poets they might want to look for, which includes the poets used for the poetry find. I want to push their thinking beyond Shel Silverstein.

Notes

I have students begin writing in their "Notes" section by answering questions on a writing-reading survey (see Appendix). Why in the "Notes" section? Because even though students' answers are their own, and as such reflect their own thinking, *I* initiated the questions. The "Response" section is meant to be a place for kids to explore their own thinking, not thinking directed by the teacher.

At the same time, I show them how to list the pages of their answers on the Table of Contents and ask them to label them "Writing-Reading Survey," so they can see how the table of contents works.

In the "Notes" section, students record any minilessons or full-length lessons I teach directly to them as a whole class. This is information initiated by me—things they need to know as writers and readers. This is a record of my direct instruction to the whole class. I added this section to their notebooks several years ago when I realized students were taking notes on random pieces of paper and promptly losing them or feeling confused about where to put these notes. By keeping them in this one section, they have a record of lessons taught that they can refer back to. It is their personal resource or reference manual for lessons focused on process, content, or conventions of language. Maintaining a table of contents helps them easily access and use this information when needed.

This system also allows me to see how well they take and apply the notes they've been given. (See the Appendix for several examples of a variety of lessons they have added to their "Notes" section.)

Vocabulary

Janet Allen, author of *Words, Words, Words*, says, "The number one way to improve vocabulary is to increase reading" (1999, 16). I agree, and it is why reading is so important to all we do. My students read books of their own choice, they read in small groups, and I read aloud short pieces or whole books to the entire class. When we do talk about and collect vocabulary, it's because I want the kids to pay more attention to it as they read.

I have found that giving kids a vocabulary list or program—memorize the words, memorize what they mean (usually in one context), take a quiz matching the word with *the* definition, and then promptly forget the word—is not very helpful. I also question the usefulness of having kids continually write their own sentences from a list of words they have seldom encountered or wondered about. I've tried doing this occasionally, always with similar results. I've given students a list of words, the sentences in which they appeared, and the definitions based on the context of the sentences. I then asked them to write their own sentences showing their understanding of the words.

Here are a few examples from my students, written after they read the words in context first, but clearly only in that one context. The words are from the book *Freak the Mighty* (Philbrick 1993). All the following sentences were written by my students.

aberration

> *I used to know a person with very high aberration. She could never pay attention in class.*
>
> *I like to aberrate because it saves time.*
>
> *Aberration runs in our family.*
>
> *VT and NH are aberrations for Vermont and New Hampshire.*

abide

> *I abide at my house in the daytime.*
>
> *Bush told the troops to abide Iraq. Where would they go anyways?*

confrontation

> *I had a confrontation with my older brother and it hurt.*
>
> *I'm a passifish. I don't really like confrontation.*
>
> *My mom is at a confrontation today. She goes to learn new teaching methods.*

postulate

> *I made sure to postulate my body when listening closely to the discussion.*
>
> *I postulated to my mom for a TV for Christmas.*

regurgitate

I regurgitated back to my car before they caught up to me.

illiterate

My little brother can't illiterate.

Guys are supposed to have bad illiterate.

divulge

On my birthday I divulged into the cake.

I told a divulge to my friend. I was so embarrassed.

trajectory

Homework is a huge trajectory between me and my social life.

I trajectored over to the window so I could look out.

fealty

In court you have to put your right hand on the Holy Bible and say a fealty.

A dog is a good fealty.

demeanor

What you just did is demeanor. You are not a very nice person.

Making mistakes as we use words is one of the ways we begin to notice the nuances of correct usage. But I don't want to reinforce incorrect usage, and asking kids to write their own sentences before they have a good hold on the words often does so. In earlier grades, many students are given lists of vocabulary and are made to do exactly this. Do they remember or use the words in their speaking or writing? Hardly. Perhaps the answer is actually a resounding *no*. They haven't met the words often enough to use them. I want kids to pay attention to new words and stronger words and to use more precise words in their speaking and writing.

Think about how small children acquire words. They hear them from the adults or older children surrounding them. I still remember my grandson, Hunter, using the word *actually* at age three. "*Actually*, Grammy, I'd rather read the dinosaur book." He did not learn that word because I taught him a dictionary definition; he learned it from *hearing* it frequently.

In our classrooms we need to make a concerted effort to *use* the words we want to give to kids. I tend to use the word *compelling* when I talk about some books. I may not give it to the kids as a vocabulary word, but each year I notice kids using the words I use in their talk or writing—especially *compelling* when they refer to certain books. Our use of stronger, more

precise vocabulary contributes to our students' learning and using those words. They make connections with how we used a word and try it out for themselves.

We need to read aloud writing that is rich in language and varied in syntactical constructions. We need to use our voices in ways that help kids make educated guesses at the meaning of some words. At times, we need to give them the definitions of the most difficult words, words that we know could prevent them from comprehending a particular text. We should discuss these words before we begin reading the text. We want them to draw meaning as a whole, not be stumped and lose understanding because of difficult or new words. I give them these words in the context in which they appear and define what they mean.

We also need to ask them to pay attention to words in their own reading and their own listening, to notice words that they don't quite have a grip on as writers and speakers but which they come across fairly often. I ask my kids to find and write down three to four words per week. This may vary from student to student and teacher to teacher.

Remember, *more* doesn't necessarily mean greater learning. When we set the requirements too high, kids figure out how to fake them. Jay and Adam's seventh-grade teacher made them find and write down twenty-five vocabulary words per week. What did they do? They each wrote two or three real definitions at the beginning of the list, and two to three at the end, and filled the middle with fake words and fake definitions. They knew full well with 125 students and the lists collected weekly, their teacher read only the first and last couple of words.

I think it is most helpful to have kids write the words in the context (sentence) in which they find them. At least we know they are seeing a word used correctly, and they will be more likely to remember the use because they are writing it down. For extra credit, I encourage them to

◆ draw their understanding of the word, if visually representing their understanding helps them remember the word better, or

◆ find the etymology or history of the word, or

◆ write their own sentence that shows they understand the way to use the word.

It's fun and useful to see how words have evolved, how sensible meanings are based on the original meaning of the root and the prefix, or a derivation from another language, or how dramatically a word's meanings have changed over time and use.

Helping kids understand why they need a better, stronger vocabulary—so they can say more precisely what they really mean and they can understand more deeply and accurately what others are trying to convey to them—will make them pay more attention to the words they choose. When the reasons for doing something make sense to them, they are able to learn much more easily.

In the Appendix there are several examples of how the vocabulary pages might look; there are several examples in the "Vocabulary" section of the actual *W-RN*, too.

I recommend teachers read Janet Allen's *Words, Words, Words* (1999), in which Allen details strategy lessons such as using word families, graphic organizers, and word walls that help kids build their speaking and writing vocabularies,.

For a more in-depth study into the ways students can explore words through integrated activities, I suggest Tom Carnicelli's book *Words Work* (2001). I still remember being a student in Tom's class devoted to word study. He was so fascinated by, and passionate about, word study that I couldn't help but delight in knowing the history, the evolution, and the use of words myself. I put together an eight-week vocabulary study for my students. Yes, you heard me correctly. Eight weeks. Day after day. All focused on vocabulary. Needless to say, they were not as fascinated as I was. (After two weeks they gave me a petition begging me to stop!) Now I know that integrating a few of those activities into the year as minilessons— not semester lessons—works much better, considering what I know about adolescents and how they learn.

Spelling Matters

I care about spelling. Kids who write for real reasons for a real audience care about spelling also. They have something important to say and they want the reader to take them seriously. But incorrect spelling is the first thing a reader notices. If it matters what the reader thinks, then it matters how hard you work to make her notice the message, not its delivery through a lack of knowledge of conventions. Spell everything correctly and the reader will notice the message, not the mistakes.

I have never found lists of spelling words presented out of context to be especially helpful to middle school kids. They do the same thing they do with vocabulary lists—memorize the word for the quiz and forget the correct spelling in their own writing. What I *have* found helpful for those who really have spelling difficulties is to organize the words that give them problems under the rules that guide their spelling. In this way kids can begin to understand the patterns of spelling with which they have trouble and, therefore, learn the related rules.

For the majority of adolescents, the problems seem to be with usage more than anything else, and trusting a computer program to catch and correct these mistakes is not especially helpful. So I ask kids to look at their edited drafts and list those words they have misspelled and I have corrected on the appropriate list or under the appropriate rule. This helps them learn what they individually need to pay attention to.

The teacher needs to go through these patterns and lists with them and show them how to use their writing to identify their strengths and weaknesses in spelling. I like to take a piece of writing from a former student or another class, without the name on it, and ask the class where on the list the misspelled words should be placed. Students find this extremely helpful. When I hand final drafts of writing back, I take a few minutes in class to make sure students add any misspelled words to their lists. These are the words they didn't pay attention to or can't seem to remember.

You might give students a cartoon or two about spelling to glue into the blank space on the page opener for the "Spelling Matters" section. Pictures and cartoons are appealing to kids and often help them remember points teachers are trying to make with them. (Every time I find a cartoon or comic strip in the newspaper or a magazine that relates to anything about reading, writing, teaching, or learning, I cut it out and put it in a labeled envelope: Reading, Writing, Revision, Editing, Poetry, etc.)

I do not give quizzes on students' spelling lists, but that doesn't mean you shouldn't. If your students learn to spell better because you do things differently, you need to do what works for you and your students. (I edit, or help them edit, their writing before they write a final draft.) On final drafts of writing my students do receive a grade for the correct conventions of language. If they don't pay attention to the correct spelling of words, it affects their final grade. When I read their *W-RN*s every two weeks, I look at the spelling section to see if they are indeed using this section to better their spelling. If you have time in class when final drafts are handed back, you can take a few minutes to make sure each student is adding the words you've identified and corrected to this list if necessary.

For kids who still struggle with spelling, I suggest Rebecca Sipe's *They Still Can't Spell?* (2003). The appendix alone is rich with valuable information to use with all students. Sipe's writing style lets us hear and understand the voices and frustrations of students as they struggle, then succeed. She includes the poem "Candidate for a Pullet Surprise," by Jerry Zar, which is worth giving to all kids to show them what a spellchecker won't do.

Variations with the *Writer's-Reader's Notebook*

The *W-RN* does not have to be used solely for the language arts or reading class. It could be incorporated into science, social studies, math, life skills, health, or world language classes. The notebook can be a place for recording data, collecting facts and questions, making predictions, sketching observations, planning labs for experiments and solving problems, conducting interviews, researching issues for an inquiry project, working out cause and effect, and gathering evidence and reaching conclusions. The notebook can be the organizational tool the teacher of any discipline uses to help her students gather their thinking, no matter what the focus. It could be used as a moon journal (Chancer and Rester-Zodrow, 1997), a nature's eye sketchbook and journal, the notebook for a wilderness adventure, a reader's log, a travelogue for a world language course, a healthy issues notebook for a wellness class . . . the possibilities are endless. The focus is observing, reading, writing, sketching—to think and question and learn. (See References, "Using a Notebook as a Nature Journal or Sketchbook.")

Even in various language arts and reading classes, each of us may use the *W-RN* differently, especially the "Response" section. Nancie Atwell (2007) no longer asks her students to write nightly or weekly entries about their reading. She asks only that they write a letter-essay to her or a classmate every three weeks about a book they have finished reading. She asks her students to revisit and skim the book, to "choose a chunk of text that [they] think shows something essential" (77) about the book. And she guides the letter-essay by saying, "[It] teaches you something you didn't realize about your book, or yourself as a reader, before you wrote it" (76–77). If I were asking my students to do this kind of writing, I might ask them to use the "Response" section to collect those passages as they read, and to write their letters back and forth right in the notebook. That could be the focus. Or it could be the focus for one quarter of the year.

When I taught seventh grade I framed the "Response" section a bit differently as a way to build their thinking and to teach the students how to read their books more closely. I would use this same frame if I were teaching sixth or seventh grade; or had a significant number of English language learners (ELLs) who needed to build their knowledge of language through more guided writing and reading connections; or had students who needed more guidance in using a writing-reading notebook. Guiding the response:

First quarter: Students' response to reading consisted only of *collecting short passages*: passages that held language that surprised, amused, angered, or confused them, or that seemed to hold significance to understanding a character or point in the book, or that touched them personally in some way. They had only to write down the passages as they read with the page number from the book. No minimum or maximum limit and no written reason for choosing the passage(s).

Second quarter: Students collected passages and explained why they chose it (see First Quarter). Having students explain why they chose the passage encouraged them to be more intentional in their selection of quotes.

Third quarter: Students collected passages, explained the meaning and significance of each passage in the context of the book, or in the context of their lives: what the passages meant to them, what they learned from them, or what the passages brought to mind for them in relation to their own experiences, or in the context of the book.

Fourth quarter: Students could continue to do all they were doing the previous quarter and were asked to think about what they took from the book as a whole and how it made them think about themselves, others, other books, and the world in which they lived. In other words, they explained what understandings about the book or the world as a whole they drew from a particular passage, or the book as a whole.

In all four quarters, I encouraged them to write anything they thought or noticed about themselves, their world, and the world at large. If kids are having trouble using the *W-RN* because the possibilities are too open-ended, I have them follow the guidelines above to work their way into more in-depth thinking as readers and writers.

If I were teaching any other class, I would have students use the "Response" section to reflect the thinking, the wondering, and the questions they had with respect to that discipline. The "Notes" section could still be used for direct instruction lessons from the teacher, and the "Vocabulary" section could hold the words vital to that course, including the academic vocabulary so essential to various disciplines.

If I were teaching a separate reading class, this *W-RN* would be the heart of all we did as readers, just as in the language arts class it is the heart of all we do as readers and writers.

Although I think we are losing something special when students type their responses instead of handwriting them (the same way we have lost the art of letter writing to instant messaging), we are gaining fluency, efficiency, and a greater chance of actually being able to decipher what is written. With students so adept on computers, it certainly may be more proficient for them to keep a *W-RN* digitally. Students could be typing their responses on the computer, printing them out, and attaching them to the *W-RN*. Or they might use the computer instead of using the *W-RN*, yet the framework and expectations could be the same, but the response may be more efficient and more in depth. In either case, it is far less cumbersome for many of our students to do this work on the computer. And it may be far more efficient for teachers as we learn to respond using technology.

Evaluation and Written Response

The *W-RN*s are meant to be academic journals that reflect students' thinking and learning as they live, act, and grow in school and the world. They are not meant to be diaries, places where kids gush out their deepest, most personal feelings, meant to be kept hidden from any and all readers; they're not meant for extremely personal writing that students will look back on and find embarrassing as they grow and mature. (Although, no matter how sophisticated their thinking is, they may be slightly embarrassed when they read their notebooks years later.)

Naturally their personal lives will at times enter these notebooks in the same way pieces of my personal life have entered my notebooks. It's impossible to totally separate their personal beliefs and feelings from their thinking as they negotiate adolescence. I don't want them to. But these notebooks are meant to be centered on who they are as *learners*.

I make it clear to the students that I will be reading these notebooks; and, on occasion, so will peers of their choice. If they feel compelled to write something in the *W-RN* that is especially personal, they can fold down the page, and I won't read it. If they write something that leads me to believe they are being hurt, or they are going to harm themselves or someone else, I am obligated both legally and morally to seek more professional help for them. They *know* this.

More than anything else we do, the *W-RN* is about "good faith participation" (Romano 1987). I believe students have to do a lot of writing to find their best writing. I believe writing helps them become better readers and reading helps them become better writers. I believe they need to be readers for the pure pleasure of a good story—without having to synthesize and analyze everything they read. I believe that talking or writing about *some* of their reading can help them unfold the layers of significance and perhaps discover authorial intention, and that the more they read and talk about their thinking as they read, the more they will discover the craft of writing. The more they read and write, the more they will learn about themselves and the world.

The writing in the notebook is first-draft thinking, a one-sided conversation students have with themselves that I am privileged to read. I nudge their thinking with my comments, questions, and suggestions, but I seldom correct their spelling or sentence structure because this is not crafted, edited writing. (You will notice this when you read the student examples in Part II.)

Because the *W-RN* is focused on students' learning, and it is an essential component of the writers-readers workshop, I read and grade all aspects of it. This reinforces that this is important work. I have also found that students want credit for all they do.

I read the notebooks every two weeks—but only one class' notebooks a day. For instance, I collect one section's notebooks every other Monday, another section's every other Tuesday, and so on. I cannot do it any more often than that, although to establish the habit of reading and writing on a nightly basis, I wish I could read these notebooks at least weekly, if not daily. But I can't. When I tried to read them weekly, it was all I did every day. I have other things to do and learn also. Every two weeks is the best I can do.

The "Response" section carries the most weight. In the course of a week, I expect to see five half hours of reading and one to three pages filled with writing, drawing, or collecting. Evidence of reading is demonstrated through recording the date, the title of whatever was read, and the time spent reading. The students count up how many half hours of reading they have done during the two-week period and note that number on the last page of the writing for the two weeks. They then count up the number of pages they have filled in the "Response" section. In a two-week period, the number should be

<u>10 </u> (half hours of reading)

2–6 (pages of writing or drawing)

This determines their *quantity* grade (time spent reading and number of pages of response). At the end of the quarter I add up the half hours of reading and the number of pages of writing. If they've fulfilled the weekly expectations each week, they cannot get below a B for the *quantity* of reading and writing. If they have done more reading and writing, they have earned an A; if they've done less, they have earned a C.

I also give the students a *quality* grade. I admit to having no rubric for this grade. It is subjective, based on my beliefs and the students' written evidence that they are reading voraciously (for pleasure and for information), that they are thinking deeply and widely about that reading, that they are paying attention to the world around them with all they notice, wonder, and question, and that they are drafting that thinking through writing or drawing. In other words, they are doing what I've described throughout this guide—collecting thoughtful and thorough responses and reactions to all they notice, and surprising me, teaching me, and challenging me with their thinking.

The quality grade is written as ✓ (C), + (B), or ++ (A). Throughout Part II, as you look at students' pages, you will see these grading notations. Most of the numbers (the quantity grades) show the amount of reading and writing a student did over a two-week period, although you are seeing only a small portion of that writing. Some students do far more than I ask; others do far less.

Frequently I will ask students to star their best thinking during the two-week period—their self-selected strongest writing or reasoning. Things they noticed, wondered. Since I believe we all need to do a lot of writing to find our best writing, then I don't need to read everything they write. When I ask them to select their best thinking, I am teaching them to self-evaluate. Their quality grade is based on this starred page or pages.

Once a month I also look for the poem they selected and their reasons for selecting it. If you look at Brian's pages in Part II you can see his selected poems and why he chose them.

What do all my squiggles, checks, and underlining on the students' pages mean? They indicate that I have read the kids' words and found something they said or the way they said it, interesting. They begin to look for those squiggles and begin to realize that if they didn't get any, maybe they need to push their thinking a bit harder and be more thoughtful and thorough in all they are doing. (Please note that many of the squiggles and lines have been removed from the samples for ease in reading and using as examples for your students.)

As an honest reader, I attempt to confirm and extend their thinking with something between a note and a letter—*I heard what you said,* and *it's making me think this.* I write notes that are quite short or questions in response to things they've written. Sometimes I feel compelled to write whole letters because I am concerned about something a student has said and feel it really deserves a more thoughtful response. All of this response is similar to the way I respond to their drafts of writing: This is what I noticed that you did well, these are the questions that popped into my head as I heard or read your writing, and here's a suggestion or two that might push your thinking.

Each time I look through the notebooks, I also check students' reading lists and put the date down the right-hand margin so I can begin to see how many books a student reads in a two-week period. In my rank book I write down the number of books the student read in that two weeks and the authors of the books.

I also check the "Notes" and "Spelling Matters" sections for how well the students have taken notes during the week and/or added spelling words to the lists. I simply note this as done or not done with a check (✓) or a zero (0). If these sections are not done, I follow up with the student to find out why she is encountering a problem with taking notes or transferring spelling to her lists.

I check the "Vocabulary" section, expecting anywhere from six to eight words during a two-week period. If they are good words (ones I think the student will begin to use in his writing and speaking the more he encounters them), I write down the number of words with a ✓, +, or ++.

My response (to the "Response" section) may be more important to the majority of the students than the grade. Kids want to know I read their notebooks. They pay more attention to my comments than they do to the grade. I have to be very careful that my comments stay positive, even when the students appear to be doing little. Encouragement is a far greater motivator than disappointment and anger. Still, in the rush to read a hundred or more notebooks during a week, I have at times written something that I know has stopped a student's reading or writing. I have to continually remind myself to pay attention to each student as an individual and to be more thoughtful about what I say to push their learning forward, not stop it dead in its tracks.

I do think we have to keep grades in perspective. When I asked students at the end of the year what helped them most as readers and writers, not one of them mentioned grades. This is what they did say:

What has helped you the most as a reader this year?

◆ having reading required each week

◆ silent reading on Fridays

◆ being made to write in the *W-RN*
> *The notebook lets me see how much I actually read.*
> *Writing about reading makes me think about what I read.*
> *The notebook helps me organize my thinking.*
> *Since I have to write in my notebook, I actually think more about what I read now.*
> *Being able to write in the notebook has really helped me with my reading. . . . If I don't understand something, then I write it in my notebook and it makes more sense.*
> *The notebook lets me see how much I actually read.*

Writing about reading makes me think about what I read.
The notebook helps me organize my thinking.

- suggestions and recommendations of good books from friends and teachers
- ability to choose authors and books that interest me
- reading more challenging books
- a quiet room
- having so many books in the classroom

What has helped you the most as a writer this year?

- conferences with the teacher
  constructive criticism
  suggestions
  I didn't know how much writing about writing could help me write.
- writing about those topics that are my own choice
  personal interest
  happened to me
  meaningful to me
  care about it
  If I write about something that really interests me, I put a lot more thought and effort into it.
- reading writing out loud so I can hear how it sounds
  My writing is much better if I read it out loud and see how it sounds.... I notice things when I hear it.
- opportunities to revise and redraft
  really lets me think about the writing
  reading it over and over so I really know if I've said what I want to say
- quickwrites help me find ideas.
- notebook writing makes me think about writing, helps me find writing
- being asked to do lots of writing, with time to do it
- computers would help

The Importance of the *Writer's-Reader's Notebook*

August 6, 1986. I read Don Murray's words:

> The most valuable writing tool I have is my daybook. . . . All the writing in the daybook
> is a form of talking to myself, a way of thinking on paper. . . . The daybook stimulates
> my thinking, helps me make use of those small fragments of time that on many days
> is all the time I have to write. There is no sign of struggle. I'm not fighting writing. I'm
> playing with writing. . . . The daybook also keeps my writing muscles in condition; it
> lets me know what I'm concerned with making into writing; it increases my produc-
> tivity. . . . [It's a place] where you can do all the bad writing and bad thinking that are
> essential for those moments of insight that produce good writing. (1990b, 10–14)

At the top of the page of a blue spiral notebook, I write, "Inspired by Don Murray's Daybook, I begin my first Reading-Writing Log." I have been keeping a writer's-reader's journal or notebook ever since. The notebooks have their own center shelf above my desk because they are so important to me. They are academic journals, where I try to record my thoughts and feelings about reading, writing, teaching, learning—observations of the world close to me or seemingly far away, ideas for writing, things that surprise me, perplex me, things that are important to me as a learner and teacher. Pictures and drawings, snippets of articles and reviews, poems and songs have crept into my notebooks over the years. What I call these collections keeps changing—from log to journal to notebook.

Although I wish I had written more about my personal life—being a wife, mother, daughter, caregiver for children, grandparents, and eventually parents; housecleaning, folding laundry; sanding woodwork, stacking firewood, mowing the lawn . . . all those personal, daily pieces of our lives that keep us working well past midnight through the weekends and up again at 5 A.M. before we go to work as teachers—I'm glad I didn't try to include everything. As an academic journal, it gives me a focus despite all the other demands on my life. By keeping it centered, I can concentrate enough to find the details in that learning and teaching. I can even trace the roots of every piece of writing I've done back to my note-books—whether it's an article about evaluation and assessment or the disconnect between mandates and what actually is good teaching, a poem or narrative about my mother's death

or the love of my grandparents, attempts at a picture book based on what I see and hear from my grandchildren, or an essay on the rewards and frustrations of keeping what I call now a writer's-reader's notebook.

As you see, my personal life *has* crept into these notebooks. I can't help it. And those moments seem more prevalent. Since 1998 my grandchildren have stepped into the pages: Hunter, Harrison, Julia, and now Fiona. Their surprises with language. Their favorite books. Their first words, first drawings, and first jottings. I can't keep them out.

I notice the same phenomenon with my students. When a student truly keeps the notebook for herself, all that's important to her creeps in. That's my biggest goal in asking students to keep a writer's-reader's notebook—that all that's *important* to them filters in because they are paying attention to the world. That world may be close to home or may broaden out to a bigger world. What's important is they are noticing the world. They are making connections. They are asking questions. They are participating by thinking.

My hope is that the notebook becomes more than an academic journal kept because of the requirement of the teacher. It is not a diary, but it does begin to hold the honest thoughts, feelings, ideas, observations, and questions of students; it becomes "a quiet place to catch your breath and begin to write" (Fletcher 1996a, 1). I want it to be a place where they are the most honest, most passionate, most thoughtful, and most thorough writers and readers they can be at these moments in their lives—whether they are ten-year-olds, or thirteen-year-olds, or sixteen-year-olds.

When the *W-RN* is working well, I get what I ask for. Pessimism. Optimism. Likes. Dislikes. Loves. Hates. Biting, cryptic sarcasm. Joy. Anger. Frustration. Delight. Confusion. Envy. Humor. Fear. Loneliness. Surprise. Boredom. With, in, and about themselves, others, their worlds, their reading, and their writing.

This is what I ask for: personal, individual, real, and so insightful.

In Conclusion

John Gregory Dunn says, "The point of a notebook is to jump-start the mind" (Murray 1990, 83). The students who take their *W-RNs* seriously know that. "Writing in the notebook makes me think," said Dylan. I want the notebooks to become a habit that Dylan, and others, will keep. Sometimes we are lucky enough to hear what our students have taken from our classes.

October 19. I am in a meeting after school and miss a visit from a former student, Emily, now a sophomore in high school, when she comes by the middle school for a visit. She leaves a note on the table.

> Dear Mrs. Rief,
>
> I've been thinking about you lots lately because I am about to come to a closure in the journal you gave me at the end of 8th grade. . . . I'm not sure if you remember the journal, but it has been a place where I have collected many thoughts and memories that I would have lost if it wasn't for these pages. I'll never forget your big black journal that you would sit and write and sketch in while we jotted down words in our notebooks during quickwrites. Your writing inspired me to write down more things than I would have ever before, and as I look back on previous pages, it's funny to see how much I've changed. . . . I just want to thank you for starting me off and for encouraging me to write. . . . I have kept writing.

Tricia, a student of mine in eighth grade more than thirteen years ago, and now a college instructor, writes me a note that finds me through the middle school email server:

> Remember how you used to have us keep reading logs? I bet you still have your students do it. I realized the other day that I've started keeping a teaching log. It started out that I'd get ideas during or after class and jot them down on sticky notes, but that wasn't very satisfactory. So I started bringing a notebook to class just for jotting ideas, etc. Now I find myself writing not just ideas for the next class, or possible ways to improve a lesson the next time I give it, but I'm venting about students and "thinking" through how to handle these discipline issues. It's great. Before I'd drive home and my mind would be racing as I went over possible ways I could have done things

better. Now I write them in the log at the end of class and move on. (*Voices from the Middle,* May, 2003).

March. I walk to the end of our driveway to get our mail. One of our neighbors is passing by and stops to chat. I catch up on the current news about her three adult children, all of whom I've had in class. The talk turns to Mike, her youngest, a third-year law student in California. He has just returned from a semester interning at the International Criminal Tribunal for Rwanda in Arusha, Tanzania. "I hope he kept a journal," I say, rather expecting that he probably did not.

"Oh, absolutely," his mom says. "His room at home is still filled with all the journals he's kept since middle school. He's forbidden me to look at them. And I haven't . . . even though it's quite a temptation."

I ask if she thinks Mike would mind my writing to him. "He'd probably love to hear from you," she says and gives me his email.

Here's his response to the email I sent:

Mrs. Rief,

It's very nice to hear from you. My parents did tell me that you might be contacting me about your book on journal writing. Without further ado . . . [Mike was always one to get right to the point!]

I don't remember when I started keeping my journals, but I'm pretty sure it was sometime in middle school. I have been keeping them ever since fairly regularly.

What I write about depends on why I'm writing. Most of the time I write just to get stuff out. It's kind of strange, I just turn my conscious brain off and let my fingers start typing and see what comes out. Other times I write because I want to remember things that I am afraid I will forget—impressions, events, anecdotes, ideas, my neighbor's dog trying to attack me every time I went for runs in the neighborhood during my teenage years, etc. [Oh no, I think that was our dog!]

The form and content of my entries (from middle and high school) probably haven't changed much. I wrote about what was on my mind then and I write about what is on my mind now. I'm sure my writing itself is probably better now, but the essence is the same. If anything, the entries have gotten less formal and more free-flowing over time. In real life I think I write pretty clearly with a lot of short sentences and paragraphs. My journal entries are usually just one really long paragraph with long sentences.

I do look back on my previous entries from time to time. What I notice the most is that sometimes I was so right about predicting/describing/analyzing people/places/life and other times I was so wrong. It's humbling in a way.

All the entries make sense to me. I still can relate to the person that I was when I wrote them.

I wrote more than usual in Africa because everything was so new, different, and exciting. I wanted to record my thoughts about everything and everyone, so a lot of my entries were about my first impressions. I also wrote about the little stories and details that I thought were funny or illuminating that I was afraid I would forget.

I hope all is well with you and your family.

For Emily, Michael, and Lil, whom you will meet in the Afterword, keeping a journal or notebook is a habit, one they have kept since eighth grade. For Tricia, it is a habit she has found again. Each of these young people has made the notebook his or her own, filled with what matters most at the moment. For them it is a place to *catch their breath* and figure out what they notice and are thinking about themselves and the world. They are paying attention. It is just what we hope for all of our students when we hand them a writer's-reader's notebook.

In *Lasting Impressions* (1992), Shelley Harwayne writes about literature as being a metaphor for keeping a writer's notebook. She says, "in Norton Juster's *Phantom Tollbooth*, Alec speaks to Milo in the land of Discord and Dynne. He is describing a telescope, but he might be referring to a writer's notebook" (133).

"Carry this with you on your journey," he said softly, "for there is much worth noticing that often escapes the eye. Through it you can see everything from the tender moss in a sidewalk crack to the glow of the farthest star—and, most important of all, you can see things as they really are, not just as they seem to be. It's my gift to you." (Juster 1961, 132)

When our students recognize the *W-RN* as a *gift*, we know they have made it their own, and, like Emily, Tricia, Michael, and Lil, they just might find it important enough to keep it in their lives beyond our classrooms.

PART II

Student
Notebook
Samples

Student Notebook Samples

Part II contains sample pages taken directly from my students' *W-RNs*. This includes the work of a range of students, some sophisticated and motivated as readers and writers, others needing a bit more nudging to come to reading and writing often. This sampling includes students with special needs, identified with a variety of modifications, and ELL students from places such as South Korea, China, the Dominican Republic, Mexico, Bulgaria, Russia, India, and Poland.

Sometimes I chose just single pages from a student to show the depth of his or her thinking; other times I chose a number of pages by an individual so you and your students could see one student's use of the notebook over a longer period of time. Show your students as many of these pages as you think will help guide them with their choices about how to use their notebooks. Look at the examples to see what my students did to deepen their understandings of themselves, books, and the world around them. Notice my comments in response to what the students wrote. These are just samples—enjoy what your students make of their *W-RNs*.

CONTENTS

> **Note:** Matthew's writing was made more fluent through the use of starter phrases, such as "I was confused
> by . . ." Diagnosed with autism, Matthew was able to access his thinking with such prompts (see bookmark in
> the Appendix) and having someone else type his verbal response. His aide and I also noticed his thinking
> about reading deepened when he first watched a movie that gave him prior knowledge and images related to
> his reading.

> **Note:** *Sometimes our response must go beyond a few words.*

Megan

November 28
But I'll Be Back Again
Cynthia Rylant
30 minutes

"Writing stories has given me the power to change things I could not change as a child. I can make boys into doctors. I can make fathers stop drinking. I can make mothers stay"

Cynthia Rylant really thinks a lot like I do in terms of why she writes and how she writes. I like to write things that have a lot of parts of me in them, and change what really happened. I have all of the control, and I can do whatever I want. I think this may be why Cynthia Rylant writes a lot of her stories about love Because she didn't have a lot as a child. She didn't have a father or a mother, really. So she writes her stories about

✓ people who do have love, like she wishes it had been for her.

She may not have had control of her life as a child, but she has such power as a writer. Terrific that you recognize that.

©2007 by Linda Rief from Inside the Writer's-Reader's Notebook. Portsmouth, NH: Heinemann.

1. Megan: Collecting and Responding to a Passage from Cynthia Rylant

Zhiwen

afraid 11-3

☆ I am afried to go to school,
everyone goes to school for fun. But
not me.

In the Social Studies and
Science, I even don't know what
should I do. I just watching
them. They thought I am something
wrong.

In China I was a wonderful
student and I was popular. I
had so many friends in the school,
I felt like I would not ~~lonely~~
be lonely. Mom said:" Just patience."
I can't, I feel I can't stay
with Americans anymore.

I believe if a person
doesn't went to any other countries
and have never felt like can't
do anything. That person
won't knows what I'm saying
now, and never ever knows how
a ferign student feel like
            ↑foreign

Your English
continues to get
stronger.

I am so sorry
you are feeling so much fear.

You are right, no one else
understands this unless they've
experienced it.

It will get better. "Patience!"

2. Zhiwen: Personal Fears of Trying to Understand English as an ELL

This is a drawing of a Dirt Biker October 4 Mike
hitting a corner full throttle. Drawing
50 min.

You are a
terrific artist,
Mike.

When you are ridding a dirt bike you get a riding humming
wicked adrenaline rush ~~when~~ as you go huming down
the public trail. The sights are amazing ~~when~~ as (What sights?)
you ~~are pretty much~~ flying down the trails (are amazing?)
everything goes by so fast that it's freaky. The (What does
sounds are loud so loud that it makes my "freaky"
ears ring. The smells are great especially the look like?)
smells of burning gasoline from rubbing the (What does the
engine so much. The feeling is freaky when "rubbing the
you are speeding down a trail and the bike engine" mean?)
starts to shake.

3. Mike: Dirt Biking—Drawing and Writing from Experience

Sarah K.

"No words left"
All the words in the world
won't pattern into how I feel.
Every time I speak
I make my problems bigger.
Words
aren't my medium.
An ex-friend helped me realize
all the explaining + trying
to find words
can't save us from our self-rooted demise.
The crumpled pages
& torn notes
& bitter, confused good-byes
could all gang up & encircle the earth.
But still a light comes shining through—
But still
no words come to mind.
I sit down with my pallette & brush
& it feels ~~better that way~~
a little better
that way.

I think you are a painter with words! I always wonder what comes first for you — the painting or the words — because they always seem to flow into, and out of, each other. I don't think it matters — both are alive with color, shape, and feeling.

©2007 by Linda Rief from *Inside the Writer's–Reader's Notebook*. Portsmouth, NH: Heinemann.

4. Sarah K: Rough-Draft Poem—"No Words Left"

3-30   Chris

JumpingFire Murry A. Taylor   30 min
This book sofar is About
a fifty year old smok Jumper.
This book has ~~told~~ taught me
Just how hard being A smoke Jumper
really is. Right now I want to
be three things when I grow up.
They are becoming a S.W.A.t.
officer, Apache Pilot and A Smoke
Jumper. In order it would be
       Pilot, S.W.A.t., Smoke Jumper.
The Smoke Jumper some say
"Outdated" because they get
stuck in trees all the time and
Can really hurt their knees so
much ~~and~~ that Jumps can cause
Cerious damage to backs. Their is
a Job kinda like smoke Jumping these
guys repelle out of helicopters   { How is
so maybe that is safer.   { this safer?

              All three of these professions
              sound dangerous to me. what traits
              or strengths do you need to succeed
              at these?
                 Why do we need people to be able to
              rappel out of helicopters? What's their job?

5. Chris: Response to *Jumping Fire*

Devyn

Cane River   4/7

4/7
30 mins
Cane River

✶ This book is so heart wrenching! Slavery is so cruel and I hate reading this book because it's so flippin sad! These slaves get sold away from their families, whipped, and forced to do things any white person is capable of doing. I wish I could just hop into the book and smack people around a bit, knock some sense into how foolish they're being.

✶   Suzette was only 13 when she was raped by a white man. That's around my age when she had her first baby. She couldn't resist or anything because she was ordered not to scream or fight. She was forced to keep it a secret until her mother noticed Suzettes bulging belly. Her second child was from the same man, conceived the same way.
      I am sickened by the history that lies behind our country and sometimes I wish I could erase it. All of it.   You can't erase" it but you can be one who changes the future. One person at a time. Some day we may actually erase it.

6. Devyn: Response to Cane River

Laine

Oct. 3   45min

Speak

Unforgotton

Don't fake your innocence
Don't deney your so wrong
don't tell me this is an accident
I can't hear your lying song
Don't tell me that your sorry
You caused me so much pain
is it my love or my forgiveness   ✓
that your still trying to gain
Stop that knocking on my broken door
I'll never let you in
I'll show you awful things you did
but where should I begin
and clearly I don't want to
So turn around and go
don't dare ask me one more time
my answer remains.

            NO.   *Laine, this is a powerful
                        response to a provocative book!*

7. **Laine:** Poetic Response to *Speak*

Dipta

3-28

I cannot believe that people feel *↓
so much hatred toward gays. A lot of people
derive their feelings from the bible. If you
are a homosexual, you will burn in hell. Those
feelings are totally absurd. Rascism is now
faltering more than ever even though it
exists. But we look at our ancestors and ask
how could the Holocaust happen? or how come
blacks were not even treated as citizens thirty
years ago? I believe we our posterity
will look back at us in disgust. How could
our ancestors be anti- homosexual? they might
say. I don't like the idea of following the
bible literally. In it - it says if you I don't
are not Christian, you will not be accepted into understand
heaven. So all of the world's people, who are where hate
not Christian, will go to hell? I deeply comes from.
respect anyone's beliefs, but they should not We will
impose their beliefs on others. I do not know destroy ourselves
of any part in the bible that says if you are if we don't
homosexual, you cannot go to heaven. Anyway, this learn to respect
is how some parts are interpreted. People must follow differences!
what is just and morally right, not something that
was written thousands of years ago or even yesterday.
Homosexuals should be looked at as regular human
beings and should be treated as regular human beings.↑

8. Dipta: Questioning Prejudice and Hatred

Sally

3/3

<u>The Giver</u>
Lowry
4:30 — 6:00

This book made me cry. I finished...reading it and I went to my window and peered out at the crusted snow. I was so glad there was snow. I was so glad I was crying. I put my hands and my cheek against the window, and I was so glad it was cold.

What would it be like without feelings?

I am grateful that I have love, compassion, grief, anger, even hate. My life would not be worth living without feeling, color, sound, music, differences. Yes, most of all diferances. I am different from everyone else and I take pride in being different.

Sally, I think you took the most important thinking you could from Lowry's book!

9. Sally: Response to *The Giver*

Joe

⭐ I just finished reading The Greatest War the other day. That was one high quality book. It kept me on the edge of my seat for almost the entire time. There was hardly a dull moment. If the author, Gerald Astor, wasn't writing about the extremely intense periods of combat, (which he was for most of the time) he was writing about the training of the men high in command giving orders.

~~This book showed me that~~

⭐ After reading this book, when I look at an ad for the army I get reminded that behind all the glory and heroism, war is a torturuse, horifiying, gory, and terrible sad expierence.

It is wierd, sometimes I think it would be cool to go into the army. I would be able to tell great stories, and if I didn't go into combat, I would make great friends and lifelong connections.

Here is one ad for the Air Force reserves, its on the next page.

→ luckily you recognize all that's NOT said in an ad trying to convince you to do something. Now you have a more realistic version. I'm glad you're recognizing multiple viewpoints/perspectives.

11/5
Weasel

1 hour of reading

10. Joe: Comparative Response and Poem After Reading *The Greatest War*

War   Oct 31
sign-ups
draft
training
invasion
harsh
gory
sad
scary
horrifying
best friends
death
destruction
bombs
guns
bullets
ammo
K-rations
freezing cold
feet hurt
pain
terrible
~~WAR~~ !

honor
nightmares
~~war~~ !!!
dreams
WAR!

So many
conflicting
feelings about WAR!

11. Joe: Comparative Response and Poem After Reading *The Greatest War*

Aillinn

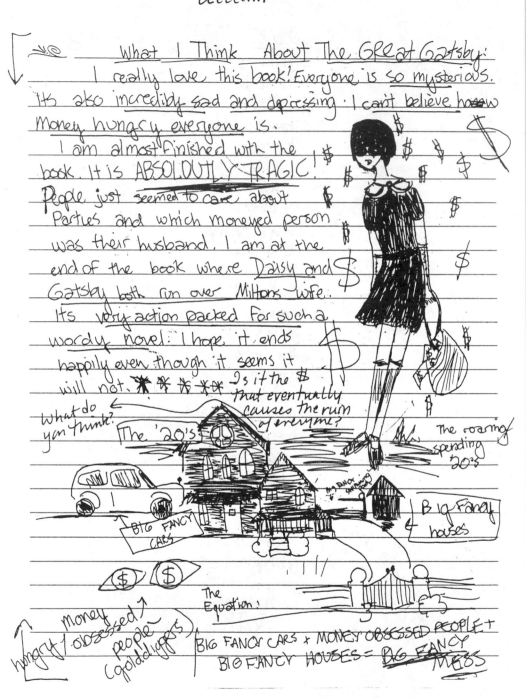

What I Think About The Great Gatsby:
I really love this book! Everyone is so mysterious.
It's also incredibly sad and depressing. I can't believe how
money hungry everyone is.
I am almost finished with the
book. It is ABSOLUTLY TRAGIC!
People just seemed to care about
Parties and which moneyed person
was their husband. I am at the
end of the book where Daisy and $
Gatsby both run over Miltons wife.
It's very action packed for such a
wordy novel. I hope it ends
happily even though it seems it
will not. ※※※※※ Is it the $
that eventually
causes the ruin
of everyone?
What do
you think?

The '20's

The roaring
spending
20's

BIG FANCY
CARS

Big Fancy
houses

The
Equation:
money
hungry / obsessed
people
(old + young)
BIG FANCY CARS + MONEY OBSESSED PEOPLE +
BIG FANCY HOUSES = BIG FANCY MESS

12. Aillinn: Playing with Sketching and Writing in Response to *The Great Gatsby*

©2007 by Linda Rief from *Inside the Writer's–Reader's Notebook*. Portsmouth, NH: Heinemann.

Sam

Of Mice and Men
1:00
2/9/01
      I started this book today. I think the relationship between George and
Lennie is so sweet. George always pretends like he doesn't want Lennie
around and gets mad at him but deep down inside he really loves Lennie. I
feel bad for Lennie because George treats him like he's four, just because
he's stupid. For example Lennie wanted to keep a dead mouse in his pocket
to pet, but George said he couldn't. When this happened I felt sad for Lennie
because he just wants something to do but George took that away from him,
I don't think I would like it if someone wasn't letting me make decisions for
myself. Also when he told Lennie not to talk when they went to see the boss
made me confused. I felt confused because Lennie is just not very smart but
he still knows how to talk and if the boss wanted to talk to him and Lennie
didn't respond I would think that the boss would be angrier. I also wonder
how Lennie and George met and how they became friends because they
seem like such an unlikely pair. Some of my thoughts were maybe they are
brothers or they grew up together and I hope that the author will reveal this.
I also wonder why Lennie is so stupid did something happen to him when he
was a kid or does he have a mental deficiency. This reminds me of the kid
from Freak the Mighty, because he was really strong but was not smart at
all.

The Giver
      I've read this book three times, yet every time I read it I learn more
and think about more. Now that it's being read aloud and there is
conversation I realize even more about the world Jonas lives in like how
unfair it is because they have almost no freedom. I think it would be awful to
live in such a "fake" world. I don't even think you are really living without
love, or good and bad feelings. Feelings are such an important part of life
that without them it is almost meaningless because living just for the sake of
living isn't fun. I don't know why people would want to go to "sameness"
and I think Jonas has the right idea wanting to reveal it to people. This book
makes me worry of a possible future like this and could the world ever
manage (or want) to do this to our world when my children or me are older
and I hope they would not consider it.
        *What feelings would you not mind
getting rid of?*
          *What in our world today makes
you think we might be headed in
this direction for the future?*

13. Sam: Response to *Of Mice and Men* (Personal Choice Reading) and *The Giver* (Whole-Class Reading)

Owen

Delta Force   60 min.

the book I've most recently
started, Delta Force, is a gruesome
tale of post-9/11 warfare. Conner
Tyler, a Delta Ranger is hired by
a deformed General to train a group
of Delta men to become America's
own set of terrorists. Their
mission- steal, destroy, kill, and anything
else to create problems within Al
Queda and the Taliban. The tests
Tyler puts his men through are gruesome,
sick, and violent and his men think him
to be a twisted man. Tyler must want
to tell the men the way he faked the
deaths of children, terrorists, and women
but he can't in order to see if the
men had the guts it took to do their
job. I couldn't have done it. I couldn't
put a gun to a man who's tied up
and pull the trigger, even though I know
it's a test. No chance. That's not what
America is supposed to be. Assasins and
terrorists are things for the countries
we fight. We're supposed to be
the overpowering diplomats who step

14. Owen: Response to Delta Force

in to end the violence —not create more terror. The very terror we wish to stop is what we must resort to to save our country? The attacks on 9/11 were horrible, and only with the images of the collapse could I pull a trigger to kill a man who can't defend himself. A man with an AK-47 aimed at me? That's different, that's war. that's a fight. This is murder, cold-blooded murder. No chance to lose the fight. No struggle. Only a pleading man at my feet and a gun in my hand. That's just not right. That's not American. that's not part of what our founding fathers fought for. It's simply the shooting a man because he didn't know enough. If that's what we must do for safety, than we are no longer the country we were. If we train our soldiers into terrorists, than we are no better than the taliban we try so hard to kill. We will have reduced ourselves to rubble.

    Owen, I hope some day that you, or thinkers like you, are in charge of the world. Maybe we'd finally learn how to get along.

Jesse

Sept 12

Just thinking about this diliberate tragedy runs shivers down my spine. Terrorists took over (hijacked the four planes full of evil and destroyed the innocent lives of many people. The simpithy and sadness from all the people and family members affected by this evil act of terror is beginning to hit me.

The simple thoughts and questions of what would I have done in this situation, and how could anyone have so much hatred are being raised in my head. I wonder how this will affect all those lives and change the way we think. I am still snooken up and scared from this Frightning act.

The day 9/11/01 will be as clear as glass to me for the rest of my life. One of my cousins who has two sons of his own (8 and 6) was in the World Trade center, on the floor above the tragic incident. His name is Ed and he was the nicest man. Ed had seen the First of the twin towers get smashed by the 767 plane. I am not aware if the evacuation was successful on his floor before the second act of terror.

Oh, Jesse, I hope he got out!

I am praying each night for all the people affected by this devistating act of evil. →

©2007 by Linda Rief from *Inside the Writer's–Reader's Notebook*. Portsmouth, NH: Heinemann.

16. Jesse: Thinking About September 11, 2001

9/12/01

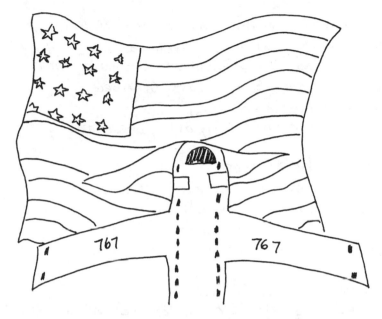

767   767

I drew this picture because I feel that this trajedy has affected the people of America. I also feel that this act of. terror will make us stronger as a country, allowing us to value what we have.

I agree. I hope it continues.

Sara

The Big Fat "F"

The teacher walks over to my desk
Her is face contorted in such a way that
fills expresses dissapointment so much that
someone might as well have stamped
"I'm dissapointed in you"
across her wrinkly, old forehead.

With her beady eyes
drilling holes in my skull
My shaking hand grabs
the sheet of paper and
labeled "Math Test".

I focus my attention
on keeping the tears hidden behind my eyes
   wide open with surprise.
My jaw drops
and takes my stomach and heart along with it,

"If you have any interest
in raising that "F"
meet me after class to discuss extra credit,"
She says.

My eyes are fixed on the red ink
The corner is smudged
I follow the "x"s down my page
and count to 5 checks
out of 30 questions

18. Sara: Poetic Response to "Math Test"

~~The~~ When class ends and it's time to go home
I race to my locker
stuffing the test in my backpack
And try to forget about it

I talk to Emily and Lauren
on the bus ride home something's
trying but ~~they~~ sense ~~whats~~ wrong
to and I'm ~~forced to~~ tell them about it
act
normal "Don't worry! Everything will be fine," Emily says.
Like "Ya, your mom will understand," Lauren says.
everything's I still don't plan to tell mom though.
I don't want her to be mad.
fine.

The bus stops outside my house
and my feet start walking
~~Off the~~ down the aisle
Off the bus
along the driveway
through the door.
I sigh with relief
when I find mom isn't home,
that she's still working.

What I wrote:
This is wonderful! What a
terrific piece of writing, even
though the subject is sad!
You create the tension well!

I'm embarrassed by
this response. It doesn't
address how badly Sara felt,
how insensitive the teacher
appeared, and how she could
craft this 1st draft.
I should have written:

Sara, I'm sorry this happened (bad grade on test, insensitive
teacher, feelings of humiliation + disappointment – self, teacher, mom–)
You capture the feelings so well. How did this happen? What went
wrong? (on the test) What did you eventually do – to tell mom, to
redo test? Now that you wrote this out, what are you thinking?

19. Sara: Poetic Response to "Math Test"

Tony

I ~~wrote~~ drew the picture on the back of
this page because its a picture of
the lead guitarist in my favorite band and
I listen to a lot of music. As you can tell that
this is Jerry Garcia because it says his name
on the picture and he has no middle finger
on his guitar hand. I give him a lot of
respect because you need your middle finger a
lot to play guitar. I know this not
because I play guitar but my brother likes
to play a lot and he's really good.

How did Garcia lose his finger? What does he/ did he have to do to compensate for the loss?

11-7
60 min
2010 a space oddysey

I like this series of books because there
written by my favorite writer (Arther C. Clark)
This book is a sequal to the book 2001
a space oddysey. I like this book because
it's packed with action, description and
imagry. I like how it is written because
it makes you think a lot when you read it.
Its more thinking than reading and I like

that because I don't like to read.

What does this book make you think about? How does it do that?

20. Tony: Illustration and Thinking About Jerry Garcia and *2010: A Space Odyssey*

← he plays in the greatful dead
Jerry Garcia

21. Tony: Illustration and Thinking About Jerry Garcia and *2010: A Space Odyssey*

©2007 by Linda Rief from *Inside the Writer's-Reader's Notebook*. Portsmouth, NH: Heinemann.

Matthew

LORD OF THE RINGS/Return of the King   1/22

I was confused by... how the ring has control over Frodo and all the things in the world.
The ring has power over the person so he wants the ring and wants to take it away and keep
it for himself. How can a ring of power control everybody? How can it rule them all, how
can it bind them, and how can it find them? Do they mean the other rings, or all the people
in the world? Is it the people they're binding or the other rings?
I wish... Golum didn't have to die to dispose of the ring. My favorite character is Golum. He
reminds me of me because I whine and mutter and I like to eat fish. I pity him because he's
such a nice person once you get to know him.
I don't see... how Golum could have gotten out of the Misty Mountains with all those trolls in
there. He doesn't have the ring so he was not invisible.

LORD OF THE RINGS/Fellowship of the Rings   1/23

I was confused because... Gandalf did not take the ring. I thought he would want to take it
because he would have lots of power. I guess the reason he didn't take it is because the
ring would overcome him if he took it. It turns you evil.
I wish... the ring could be used for good and not for evil. If it could be used for good it
might have been used to defeat Sauron and his army. Instead it needed to be destroyed.
I don't see... how the defeat of Sauron connects with the ring. Sauron was defeated when
the ring was destroyed. I don't know what the connection is between Sauron's defeat and
the ring. I think when the ring was destroyed the Land of Mordor was destroyed, and
Sauron was destroyed with it. The ring destroyed the Land of Mordor, Sauron was in it, and
he died when the Land of Mordor was destroyed.

THE SUBTLE KNIFE/Part 2, The Golden Compass   2/12

I love the way... that the subtle knife can cut through anything, any object, any matter. I
would use it to cut through gold, I would use it to cut through mountains to find gold and
diamonds. I would use it to cut through other worlds if I could.
Sir Charles reminds me of a slithering snake. He slithers around and noses into other
people's business. He tries to steal the alethiometer, he tries to put Will in jail and you
can't trust him at all. I think he has a demon up his sleeve and I think his demon is evil. Sir
Charles acts like a snake and his demon is a snake and his demon is his personality.

Friedrich [pp. 32 -64]   **March 5**

I can't believe Herr Neudorf... believes in the ways of Hitler because I believe that
teachers are not supposed to take sides. My impression when he was making the speech to
the students after school was that he was being fair to the Jews. Then he said, "Heil
Hitler!" and it sounded like he was on Hitler's side. I was very angry and surprised when he
said that. I don't know why he would have done it.
Why didn't... the woman believe Friedrich's friend when he said he broke the window? I
think she should have listened to Friedrich's friend. She accused Friedrich because he was
a Jew. It didn't surprise me that Germans treat Jews like scum because I learned it at
school. I don't think Mr. Schneider should have paid for the window. I think Friedrich's
friend should have paid for it.
I like how... Friedrich's friend sticks up for him. He admits he broke the window and he
tries to tell the officer that he did it and Friedrich didn't. The protagonist's father said he
would not participate in Mr. Resch kicking out the Schneiders when he wanted to do it
because they were Jews. I would stick up for every Jew in the world because I think what
the Germans were doing is wrong.

22. Matthew: Response to *Lord of the Rings*; *The Subtle Knife*; *Friedrich*; and *Gandhi*

Gandhi [the movie, part 1]   March 18

How did Gandhi happen to get involved in rights for people in South Africa? He got
involved when he got kicked off a train because Indians were supposed to travel third class
and he was traveling first class. He didn't move when they asked him to move. The British
thought Indians were inferior to them. Gandhi was very surprised by all the anger that the
British had towards the Indians. **But did he respond in anger?** He didn't respond in anger.
He used his brain.

**What does this mean? "His goal was freedom for India. His strategy was peace. His
weapon was his humanity." How is that different from what the British were doing?**
The British used guns, tanks, and unjust laws against the Indians. The Indians stood their
ground. The Indians were more powerful because they were for peace over war. It made
people in other parts of the world hate the British.

**How did you feel about the ways the British Empire was treating Indians in South
Africa and in India?** I think it's unfair, treating Indians like trash. I never knew about
this before. It reminds me of <u>Friedrich</u>, a book about Germans mistreating Jews.

3/20

I think THAT GANDHI IS A BEACON
OF HOPE FOR THE INDIAN NATION.
He DOes CAMPANS, SpeeCHeS, AND
FASts FOR PeACe iN tHe WORLD.

(11⁺⁺)

Matthew, you are reading
such a wonderful range of books:
nonfiction (true) and fiction (made
up from facts and the author's
imagination). I'm glad having
questions helps you talk about all
these books make you think.
   Nice to see your thinking
in your handwriting too. I know it
takes you time — so I'm impressed
you want to do that also. Whatever
you do, I see what a thoughtful
reader you are.

23. **Matthew:** Response to *Lord of the Rings*; *The Subtle Knife*; *Friedrich*; and *Gandhi*

Ryan

| Johnny Tremain 5 hours | Johnny Tremain 2 hours |

☆

Finally, a book that I REALLY get hooked to. Could it be the plot, the descripton, the adventure, or the growth of the charactor to a talented Silversmith, to a begger, and then to a skilled hourse rider. At first I was resented to read this book because in the 5th grade, I saw the movie in class, and even then I thought it sucked. But as I read the book I find it cool how there's like thousands of sub-plots such as will Johnny ever recover from his burn? will he ever find a family? and will he be a real part of the Sons of liberty?

Ryan, I'm so glad you finally found a book you like. I look forward to hearing what you think of this book once you're done.

14 halfhours

Terrific! (++)

24. Ryan: Response to *Johnny Tremain*; Illustrated and Written Response to Reading About World War II Tanks

Comparing

M-4 Sherman Tank

This tank was the bulk of American Armor, despite it's lack of armor (three inches), and fire-power (75-millimeter cannon). The German tanks however, had around a cannon of 88-millimeters and armor about 6 inches thick. The reason why the US produced such light tanks was that unlike the enemy, they had to cross an ocean to ship a tank to the battle-field. Despite its lack of combat skills, their were some possitive features to the Sherman, such as: For every four shermans made, one German tank was made. This was because Shermans were a much simpilar disign than most German tanks. And the positive trait was speed: The Sherman could go 40

25. Ryan: Response to *Johnny Tremain*; Illustrated and Written Response to Reading About World War II Tanks

the odds

Kilometers per hour, while the German tiger, a much better combat tank, could go only 32 kilometers per hour.

Terrific drawings!

Panther tank

This German terror was the main tank in the German army before the even greater fered tiger tank arrived. It was the most heavily armed tank of its time, an 88-millimeter cannon and most likly, the Mg42, the best machine-gun- available. Thankfully, these Iron beasts couldn't with-stand the much better trained and better equiped GI's.

How did these tanks perform in WWII battles? Did they change outcomes?

26. Ryan: Response to *Johnny Tremain*; Illustrated and Written Response to Reading About World War II Tanks

Seth

Hiking over the summer

I went hiking in the beatifull White ^(mnts) National Forest StatE Park. Truly a hikers play ground. ~~Filled with Notches, reviens, valleys, ice cold rivers~~ Filled with Steep, imortal notches, adrenalum rushing raviens, And the jewl of the park which are its mountains, when you reach the summit eighther an 2,000 footer or a 5,000 footer, you get ★ \|(the greatest feeling, that even the richest man in the world cant buy! And when you complete your descend you think of yourself and the world around you differently.

In only three days, I was knumbing my toes in the Swift River, discoring crystal clear water falls, such as Winnawetia falls, and Zealand falls, and hiking to Huts in the middle of beatifull settings, wher they gladly offer you lemonade, and ice-tea, as. if the alpine air wasnt sweet enough.

I walked up the water fall (Arethusa falls) as if someone or Something was call ing me. I was beeing pulled up the water fall like metal next to a magnet and when I reached the top it was the most beatifull thing I have ever seen, it was more than worth it. I saw light green mountains as far as the eye could see. It was strange because no one would ever think that ther would be another beatifull thing on top of another beatifull thing! →

27. **Seth:** Thoughts on Hiking the Swift River and Reading *Adventure New England*

Sorry for the absance of my writting in my journal, Mrs. Reif gave me a Book, "Adventure New England" by: Diane Bair and Pamela Wright wich has inspiered my writting soul to be revealed once again. And as I read about her adventures in the cold, snowy White Mountains, she strickly advises you to take a warm mummy bag, and as I write this   my body is being toasted to perfection in my own warm mummy bag!

I never finished Alive, I forgot about it because of all of my science homework. But I was still doing my nightly reading. I was reading the "Boy Scout Handbook", and there's nothing that spectacular about it, I just read the requirments I need to know to get my class's signed off. The Boy Scout book has a very dull scence of writing very unlike Pamela and Diane! "Sometimes you need to splash the soul with wonder awaken your senses with a touch of wilderness."...

I cant wait to read the next page of this book, so I'm going to have to put a period here. ☺

P.S. I think this book will inspire me to write great pieces of writting.

What if you rewrote the handbook in a more compelling way as an Eagle Scout project? You know how to "awaken" the senses through writing!

28. Seth: Thoughts on Hiking the Swift River and Reading *Adventure New England*

Emiliano

Tues. 17 Sept

My pants fell down
while I was playing
football.

"Eleven" by Sandra Cisneros

"I put one arm through one sleeve of the sweater that
smells like cottage cheese."

A girl named Rachel has her 11th birthday spoiled when a
mean teacher insists that a gross sweater belongs to her
and makes her wear it.

29. Emiliano: Illustrated Response to Personal Narrative on Football; "Eleven"; *Freak the Mighty* (Whole-Class Reading); and *It* (Personal Choice Reading)

RUN!!

Great drawing! I'm beginning to recognize your "voice" as an artist.

I drew this picture because it stuck on my mind. It's Kevin on top of Max and they're running.

Nightly Response

"It" is one of the best books I've ever read, and I'm not even half done with it. The images brought to your head by the words in the book are incredibly descriptive and radiant. The terror is very realistic too. The kids in the story are very well described and they all have very different and contrary personalities. The book is about these six kids that have one thing in common. They all see this monster that takes the shape of a clown mostly, but sometimes it takes shape of their worst fears.

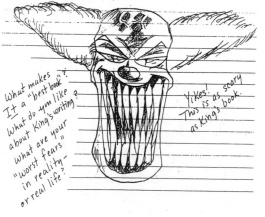

What makes it a "best book"? What do you like about King's writing? What are your "worst fears" in reality—or real life?

Yikes! This is as scary as King's book.

30. Emiliano: Illustrated Response to Personal Narrative on Football; "Eleven"; *Freak the Mighty* (Whole-Class Reading); and *It* (Personal Choice Reading)

Ania

9-16
Shabanu
2:00pm 5:00 P.m.

↓   This book is about a girl my age living in Pakistan, who is going to marry a 16 year old boy.

She lives in a male dominated society where she is taught to obay. Shabanu tells about the changes she's going through and her envy of her sister Phulan. Her whole life is pretty much planed for her.

The Pakistanian life of a women has not changed for hundreds of years, for shabanu this way of life is normal because she's been thought since she was a child that she will never be equal to a man. I respect their culture traditions and customs but by my standards their way of life is extremly shavinistic. This may seam normal to them because they've been thought this all their lives and they don't know any better.

the women have never been treated as equals so they are afraid to speak of because they'd be punished or even killed. They were made to belive that they need a man to have a happy life. Basicaly their whole life revolves around marrige.

With low standards pakistaniens lead a simple yet fufilling life. They are not educated or materialistic but they are happy because they take plesaure in symple things like emotion and familly. This is the good part of their society, they don't need money to have joyful lives.

31. Ania: Thoughts on Shabanu; Somehow Tenderness Survives; and Country Lovers

Many people think that our technology and our greed of money create the problems of this society and that without them our wories wold be gone and we could live much less stressful lives. I don't agree. This book shows that life without education and taxes isn't any less hard to live. Only in a place like the desert you can actualy realize that the line between life and deth, good and bad isn't as thick as we make it out to be. Life in the desert is as fragaile as the sunset, one minute it's there, the next, it's gone.

Shabanu and her family face problems each day, They worry if they'll have enough water to last them untill the monsoon seson. They live in fear of sand storms and scorpions, things that wouldn't even pass our minds, things that we don't have to deal with living in our safe and protected enviornment.

Desert nomads depend on nature more than anything in their lives because everything they have comes from nature and can also be taken away by it. Family is also a big part of their lives. Each family member is codependant on another for love and support. In our modren society we've drifted away from these things, that is why there is so much depresion in this world, people arn't satisfied with what they have because they always want more. They can't apreciate simple things like love and family because they think that the more they have the happier they'll be, but that is realy not the way it is. the less you have the more you apriciate it.

©2007 by Linda Rief from *Inside the Writer's–Reader's Notebook*. Portsmouth, NH: Heinemann.

32. Ania: Thoughts on *Shabanu*; *Somehow Tenderness Survives*; and *Country Lovers*

Ania, this is a beautiful poem in itself. Where were you? Who with? What has happened since then?

10-23

*☆ I remember we used to make sand casles, chase chickens, ride the dog, feed green clovers to the sheep, look at the stars at night, pick dandylions in a feald then brade them into crowns. I remember when we walked berefoot along the path of the stream trying to chase the little silver fish that swam with the current. I charish what I remember.

☆ Crackling Day
   Peter Abrahams

Somehow Tenderness
   Survives   2:00 - 4:30

☆ I was out raged with this story. As I read, I really just couldn't belive that those things realy happened, but subconscious in my subconcience I knew they have. I found myself not able to accept the kind of hostile racisim that exists to this day. I guess that how I was brought up gives me that disbelief. When you are denied the whole truth, you are blinded by those who try to protect you.

Yes!{

prejudice

   The discriminating prejedust of this story rises rage within me. I can't handle the fact that people actualy thought that one race is supirior to another; and that some still do. That sadns me, it makes me wonder how evolved the humman race realy is. We can't even endure the basic prinsipal of justice and equality.

   I presume to be intolerant to the unbarable angu wish that comes from the infliction of sufferring twards other beings, yet I become more passive as I observe it daily. But, inspite of everything, you can't become fully imune to that emotion, even though you might be able to withold it. It's just one part of being human.

©2007 by Linda Rief from Inside the Writer's-Reader's Notebook. Portsmouth, NH: Heinemann.

33. Ania: Thoughts on *Shabanu*; *Somehow Tenderness Survives*; and *Country Lovers*

Ania, this is an extraordinarily beautiful ⊕(28/26)^(++) notebook. Your response to <u>Shabanu</u> is especially thoughtful. You don't have to write so much in summary as you did in the Stephen King novel. Remember, only enough to help me see how you connected with it.

In <u>Shabanu</u> your thinking about appreciating the little things in life really struck me. We are so materialistic and seldom appreciate the natural gifts in life: sunrise, clean water, fresh air,... Have you read!

The Power of One - Courtnay?
or Phantom - Kay?
I think you <u>would</u> like both.
You may not <s>like</s> them - there will be parts that <u>outrage</u> you - but you will see great courage despite such adversity.

<u>Country Lovers</u>
Nadine Gordimer

★ This story proves that love can go beond race, but it can't suppress racism. The white boy and black girl in this story had great effection twards each other but in the world they lived in that was unheard of. They sneaked back and forth hoping that they wouldn't get caught. This made me think of Romeo and Juliette. Their love for one another was also unjustified. But they paid a greater price for it, their lives. That was pretty tragic, but this story also ends unfortionetly. When the black girl has a baby by him, he kills it as not to shame his whole family. In my opinion, what he did was self-centered.

Oh, how sad!

34. Ania: Thoughts on *Shabanu*; *Somehow Tenderness Survives*; and *Country Lovers*

Mike

$$\begin{array}{l} 4/28 - 4/30 \\ \text{Guardians of the West} \\ 3\frac{1}{2} \text{ hrs.} \end{array}$$

May 1   Romeo + Juliet

I thought the production was entertaining, not good. It was funny at parts, the fights were good, but it wasn't really Romeo + Juliet. I liked the acting of Romeo + Mercutio, even though it was somewhat overdone. I was surprised how the actors interperated some of the lines, for example when Juliet says "what's in a name, it's not arm, nor foot... nor any other part belonging to a man." I <u>do not</u> think that Shakespeare was talking about that part of a man that is above the thighs but below the waist! I did not like how the actors performed toward an audience of what they thought teens would be, sex-driven maniacs. They thought the only way we would enjoy a love story is if it is filled w/ sexual jokes, gestures, and comments. This made me a little P.O.'d.

I agree— I think they went a bit "overboard" and we lost the essence of the story!

©2007 by Linda Rief from Inside the Writer's-Reader's Notebook. Portsmouth, NH: Heinemann.

35. Mike: Response to *Romeo and Juliet* and the Author David Eddings

I didn't know Eddings wrote so many books. If you list the reading times side by side, you'd have more pages on which to write i.e. (id est = that is 😊)

5/1
King of the Murgos
By Eddings
3/4 hr.

5/2
King of the Murgos
1 1/4 hrs

5/1 King of the Murgos   ←— side by side —→   **5/3**
3/4 hr.   King of the Murgos
                                            1 hr.

5/4
King of the Murgos
1 1/2 hrs.

☆Man, David Eddings is awesome!
I have started up reading his
books again and I can't stop.
For a stretch over vacation,
I forced myself not to read
his last ~~suies~~ series. I did
not want to finish all of Eddings
books, because once I was done
with them, there wouldn't be
anymore. I knew if I started
the series I would just keep
reading them quicker and quicker

36. Mike: Response to *Romeo and Juliet* and the Author David Eddings

until there weren't anymore.
My parents thought I
had gone bananas;
that I loved an author
so much I refused to read
him. Actually, now that I
think about it, it is a little
weird. I just cannot convince
myself that there could be
possibly be another author I
enjoy as much as Eddings.
        My solution to my dilemma
is that I can only read 2-3
chapters before I go to sleep (that's
when I usually read). This way
I read the books, but I
read them slower and prolong
my enjoyment. Although usually this
works, sometimes I hit a real
good part of the book and
read for two hours. This severly
ticks off my parents because
they are avid believers
in an early-to-bed-early-to-rise
policy, and reading late on school
nights infringes on that policy.
        I wish I had found an author
I loved so much as a 14-yr.-old
that I would ban myself from
reading him or her to savor the books!

37. Mike: Response to Romeo and Juliet and the Author David Eddings

Nick

today I felt frustrated trying to explain to another WUNH DJ the style, sound and feel of John coltrane's music. coltrane is probobly the best saxophonist to ever live and has one of the most unique styles of any musician. The only way I could make him understand was to play the music for him. comming home I was still looking for a way to describe in words what only coltrane could express in music. I looked through the various CD Jackets trying to find an explanation of coltrane's sound. the best came from Charles Lloyd, another sax player. I also found many acounts of how coltrane would always be practicing.

my sax teacher once told me about a time when he went to see him play at a club in N.Y. during the break coltrane went into the bathroom and practiced. My sax teacher just watched him not wanting to interupt. "It way like he was in another world" he said.

38. Nick: Explaining His Love for the Music of John Coltrane

Feb. 20

★ " Coltrane played in fits of stops and starts — there would be flashes — then silent night."
   —Charles Lloyd

"John [Coltrane] usually showed up an hour before the [recording] session, much in the manner of classical musicians practicing before a recital. He would stand in the corner, face the wall, play, stop, change reeds, and start again. After awhile he would settle on the mouthpiece and reed that felt most comfortable to him, and then he would start to work on the "runs" that he wanted to use during the session. I would watch him play the same passage over and over again, changing his breathing, his fingering, and experimenting with the most minute changes in his phrasing. Once in awhile he would go back to a mouthpiece he had abandoned earlier.

He never lost control: Every step had a reason, and almost everything he played was acceptable to everyone but him."
   —Tom Dowd

39. **Nick:** Explaining His Love for the Music of John Coltrane

16 November

Dear

I'm sorry you experienced such terrible feelings: "anger, shame, fear." I agree, the report card was not good, and certainly not reflective of all you are capable of in so many ways.
I am also glad you didn't carry through with some of the things you were thinking: the swearing at your parents, the use of the pocket knife.
life is so precious. We only have one. It's one of the reasons I hope you think about the quote I gave you from Mary Oliver, "What is it you plan to do with your one wild and precious life?"

Now, let's think about all your strengths—things you do well. From the little I know about you, I'm impressed with your command of the English language. Do you know what a gift you have, the ability to speak English and   fluently? Amazing. So many opportunities will exist, be available to you. You are also an artist, able to communicate lots through your drawings and sketches. And you are a very fine reader—able to take significant information and meaning from all that you read—be it fiction or texts. And I barely know you. I can only imagine the other things you have strengths and gifts in.

Now let's think about the anger, and shame, and fear. Where does each come from? Do you feel the anger toward yourself, yet show it toward your parents. Their yelling and anger at you comes from wanting the best for you. Wanting you to succeed, to do well. They are disappointed, and perhaps don't have the most effective way of showing this toward you by yelling and throwing the card on the floor. You know that response doesn't work. And you held back, kept yourself from lashing out and screaming and yelling. It's the anger at yourself. The shame that you know you could have done so much better but perhaps didn't put in the effort. You are a very capable young man—who knows what to do and how to do it. You know you just need to take responsibility for that. And that may be where the fear comes in. Fear for not knowing what will become of you if you don't show and do all you can do. Fear of someone sending you back to   Fear of losing the friends you have. Fear of doing something you would regret: speaking inappropriately to others, hurting yourself.

You have to think about and figure out, what is it that's "given" you that less than stellar report card. How did that happen? What did you not do and could have done? What could you be doing differently? How could you prove to yourself you are a very capable young man who has been given an extraordinary opportunity to make the most of his life and all it offers you—your parents, the school, your friends. And speaking of your friends. Who are your real friends? The ones who encourage you to be all

40. Mrs. Rief: Letter in Response to a Student's Entries About His Disappointment in Himself and Reaction from His Parents to His Poor Report Card Grades

you can be? Who help you work seriously and productively? Not the ones who think you are funny and goof off and keep you from working?

You are the only one who can take responsibility and turn this shame and anger and fear around. Start with remembering who you are, what you are good at, and all you have to offer to others. Think of the opportunites you've been given, and the way you have so much to offer others with all you've learned, and know, and can do. Perhaps an apology to your parents, for understanding why they react the way they do. Perhaps an apology to yourself for not making the most of every opportunity. Perhaps some ideas to yourself about why each grade in each subject was what it was and notes to yourself in writing about how you can turn this around.

And lastly,   , I want you to know that note in your Reader's-Writer's Notebook ·is one of the most touching, compelling pieces of writing I have ever read. It is one of the strongest voices and so powerfully written. When you write from the heart, about those things that really matter to you, you have a voice that needs and wants to be listened to. You are not a failure at school, nor are you a failure at life. You are an extraordinary young man who will figure out what to do with his "one wild and precious life."

Mrs. Rief

41. Mrs. Rief: Letter in Response to a Student's Entries About His Disappointment in Himself and Reaction from His Parents to His Poor Report Card Grades

Sarah B.

The Catcher in the Rye   11/19
by J.D. Salinger
    2 hrs.

Ha! I read almost the whole book in
one sitting. I don't know why, because
the book wasn't even that great. I
don't understand why the book is
a classic. NOTHING HAPPENS. It's about
this rich bratt who doesn't want to
go home because he's been kicked out of
this prep school, AGAIN. The whole book,
all he does is COMPLAIN about how
he hates society, how he hates people.
Sometimes I think what he has to say
is very interesting, other times you just want
to slap the brat across the face.
        The kid swears a lot and does
things I'd never write down even at
home, but anyway... I liked the
relationship with his sister. How he
could talk to her and she'd understand.
she was only 10 years old. He kept
bringing up this girl Jane, who
was his best friend when they

42. Sarah B: Response to *The Catcher in the Rye*; *Treasure Island*; and the Movie *The Wave*

were kids. I guess that's why I read the book all at once. I thought he'd meet her and she'd be really weird or something. She never showed up though. There was this 'thing' in the book that made you feel like something was going to happen, but it never did.

Overall, it was an empty book, with a rich-brat who had a chip on his shoulder — in my opinion some people obviously like it for it to be a classic.

Why do you think it's been called a classic? What could sustain its popularity?

Treasure Island by Robert Louis Stevenson
1 hr.

I have seen versions of this book in different movies and I read the Great Illustrated Classics book when I was seven. I even read the first chapter on the internet. Now that I'm finally reading the book I think it's a book you really get into. One of those books you pull out whenever you have nothing to do.

I like how Mr. Stevenson basically tells you that Long John Silver is a pirate without actually writing it out. It's kind of funny how it's so obvious to the reader, but the characters all think Silver is an

43. Sarah B: Response to *The Catcher in the Rye*; *Treasure Island*; and the Movie *The Wave*

Island. The ending was really wierd. At the
end Trewlery and Smullet ended up being the
'bad guys' and Long John Silver became
good. I didn't like it because it destroyed
the whole theme of the book. I like
the ending when Silver sinks in the
dingy with all the treasure because he's
greedy. It's about how the pirate got
exactly what he deserved.

↙ Nice drawing!

silver tries to escape at the end

44. Sarah B: Response to *The Catcher in the Rye*; *Treasure Island*; and the Movie *The Wave*

My favorite part about this book is how fast and exciting it is. I keep wondering, "What about the treasure?" I have a feeling that will be the next issue.

My favorite character is Long John Silver because he's witty. He's ontop of himself, and he stays calm no matter what. The first impression you get of him was when he was lying to Hawkins in the bar.

⟨12/19⟩ ++

What a pleasure to read + view your thinking! I love all your sketches!

You've been reading an extraordinary range of books. Have you read:
The Diary of a Young Girl: Anne Frank

Where the Heart Is - Letts
Ellen Foster - Gibbons
Speak - Anderson
Stargirl - Spinelli
A Time for Dancing - Hurwin
A Tree Grows in Brooklyn - Smith
My Sister's Keeper - Picoult
April 13 The Wave

In the beginning, Mr. Ross was a good person who wanted to affect the lives of every kid. When Lorie asked a question, he really wanted to answer his students. Mr. Ross changed in the end. He was more assertive and seemed caught up in his own game. He started dedicating a lot of his time towards the wave. When his girlfriend told him

45. Sarah B: Response to *The Catcher in the Rye*; *Treasure Island*; and the Movie *The Wave*

©2007 by Linda Rief from Inside the Writer's-Reader's Notebook. Portsmouth, NH: Heinemann.

he should stop the wave he became angry and frustrated.

    Mr. Ross learned a lot through his own lesson. He learned how easy it is for someone not to follow the crowd, but be the leader of the crowd. He got so caught up in it, he almost let one of his students get hurt. When he'd realized what was happening he showed his students that they too had become so obsessed.

    I think Mr. Ross hadn't really planned for the wave to go as far as it did. I think he planned to get the kids caught up in the club and then show them how they had followed the crowd too easily. I don't think that Mr. Ross meant to get caught up himself. When Mr. Ross realized how much fun he was having and how organized and respectful the students were to him, he didn't want to stop the wave. He might have also been afraid the kids would be upset.

    The character that I would be most like is David. I think that I would join in the beginning because it seemed fun. It's really easy to do something that everyone else is doing, especially if it's being led by a teacher. Even Lorie was caught up in the game at the beginning. I don't think I would get so caught up that I'd

46. Sarah B: Response to *The Catcher in the Rye*; *Treasure Island*; and the Movie *The Wave*

want to hurt my friends though. I would probably just be upset at someone that was against the wave.

I don't really understand the purpose of the wave. They didn't really stand for anything other than "strength for discipline." I think it would be kind of hard for ~~everyo~~ something as meaningless as "the wave" to hurt people. I don't really understand what they stood for other than everyone being the same.

I also don't think that some parts of this movie were realistic. The actors weren't all that great and kids said a lot of things that kids would never say. "Mr. Ross, I'm very happy to be apart of the wave." But overall I think it had a good message of how easy it is to follow a group. But I definately know that that movie was no acadamy award-winner.

You really thought hard about this movie.

<u>Where the Heart Is</u>   4/17
By Billie Letts
30 minutes

" ...~~wher~~ ^{When} did Americus go down?"
"About an hour ago, but it was a struggle."
"Too excited about the snow?"
"Too worried about the animals. She was scared they'd freeze. Wanted me to fix them some soup. 'Give them a hot meal,' she said."

← What did you like about this dialogue? What does it tell you about the characters?

Can't wait to hear what you think of this book!

©2007 by Linda Rief from *Inside the Writer's-Reader's Notebook*. Portsmouth, NH: Heinemann.

47. Sarah B: Response to *The Catcher in the Rye*; *Treasure Island*; and the Movie *The Wave*

Kaitlin

9/19
Responses to the Aquarium trip
Observations of Jellyfish:

Their bell-shaped heads like a bubble
blown by a child,
So perfect and delicuite, strands of
Angel hair sweep gently—
in a current like a wind in late summer
Reflections play upon the lumniscent
bells from glowing blue lights,
And the Jellyfish dance,
bathed in their dim light above and
below them,
for they have no boundaries, no limits.
They repeat their movement, and I
know not why.
But why reason out something
glorious, if bewilderness is part of its
beauty.

*Kaitlin, did you write this? It's beautiful.
Your words move like the jellyfish – they
sweep gently across the page.*

48. Kaitlin: Range of Writing and Sketches from Field Trip to Aquarium (Jellyfish); Whale Watch; Hike ("Clover Bed" Poem); *One Child*; *The Giver*; and Mountain Hike ("Children of the Mountains" Poem)

10/6 - Whale Watch

As I watched the water where a humpback whale had surfaced a moment earlier, a glow of green was spotted in the water. The whales belly. Then, with a thrust of strength, the whale heaved it's body out of the water, stayed for a moment, and fell with greater speed. It's impact raised a thunder clap sound, and waves of water pushed themselfs out of the way. What a magnific-ent creature!

Beautiful description!

I though that that one great glance at a whale was enough for the entire trip. The whales were magnificent!!!

One time every couple of years is good enough for my stomache, though.

I learned a lot about the Isles of Shoales, and a lot more about whales. I thought the naturalist was very good. A lot of terms I missed at the slideshow were used during the trip, which I was glad of.

I think that seeing the whales in the wild really gives you an idea of how great they are.

Even being sick (I didn't throw up) was okay after seeing the mother and baby whale. It was wonderful!

I wonder if all the kids who were sick would agree!

I agree!

49. Kaitlin: Range of Writing and Sketches from Field Trip to Aquarium (Jellyfish); Whale Watch; Hike ("Clover Bed" Poem); *One Child*; *The Giver*; and Mountain Hike ("Children of the Mountains" Poem)

Clover Bed
Kaitlin

What a misty bog
this morning is
I sit on
clover beds
and ferns.

A trickling stream
along with gusty breezes
fill my ears-
and heart
with contentment.

The moss is soft
as an animal's fur
so welcoming
on a wet day.

Cloudy skies
and chance of storm
dirty face and feet
ahhhhh!

50. Kaitlin: Range of Writing and Sketches from Field Trip to Aquarium (Jellyfish); Whale Watch; Hike ("Clover Bed" Poem); *One Child*; *The Giver*; and Mountain Hike ("Children of the Mountains" Poem)

★ ★

Have you ever noticed how you always think when you grow older, you'll do things a different way?
I used to believe that I would wear red lipstick and dye my hair blue every day as a grown-up. I thought I'd live in a purple house with pink hearts, and drive a green car with purple spangles. I dreamed of the day when I'd meet a man at a prom and we would have 3 sets of twins - all girls.
But now..... those things don't QUITE appeal to me anymore!,

↑ I can't imagine why! You are so funny - imagine this place as a picture!

(1/18)
One Child
Torey L. Hayden
30 min.

I think that this is one of the most emotional books I've read. Every joy Torey a Sheila had was fragile, like a weak berry branch in a heavy storm.
It showed me how very precious love is. You can't live with it, can't live without. I really believe that.
I finished this book standing in the bathroom, and cried. My mom, who had been passing by, asked if I was okay and spoiled the moment.
It seems like every book I read that has been suggested by you or Sarah has been great!
I can't wait until I can read Tigers Eye, the sequel.

★ Isn't it interesting that we almost like being sad - or scared · maybe because it's not real? what do you think?

★ I'm so glad you liked it even though it made you cry.

---

51. Kaitlin: Range of Writing and Sketches from Field Trip to Aquarium (Jellyfish); Whale Watch; Hike ("Clover Bed" Poem); *One Child*; *The Giver*; and Mountain Hike ("Children of the Mountains" Poem)

The Giver
Response:

If no one could have their own choices, and they were protected from anger, fear, and pain, how could one ever understand joy, ⊛ excitement, and positiveness? ~~If~~ you cannot have an especially great day, because then a normal day would become a bad day. It wouldn't work. Sameness could not be achieved.

I think that I would miss music the very most if I had to live in a world of sameness. Music is color and joy, which demands, whispers, and tickles, the back of your mind.
at

I love the way you said that—"whispers and tickles..."

Response:

In life, we have to make choices and risks. The risks which turn out good are worth going through the bad ones.* If I had a giant basket of candy every day, for one thing, I'd get very sick, but for another, the candy would not be very special anymore.

I wonder if this is why we seem so nonchalant to violence and hunger and poverty and war—because we see so much of it on TV that we have become immune to it—no longer shocked! What do you think?

52. Kaitlin: Range of Writing and Sketches from Field Trip to Aquarium (Jellyfish); Whale Watch; Hike ("Clover Bed" Poem); *One Child*; *The Giver*; and Mountain Hike ("Children of the Mountains" Poem)

*Mt. Garfield (6th mountain)
(not the cat!)
Kaitlin

On the top of the mountain is a foundation
you can rest in. from this point this morning,
I can see all we've climbed:

KEY
⛺ = shelter
🏠 = hut
☁ = cloudy summit
1-5 = rating

On one side of Garfield is a view of rich mountains. The other is a view of flat civilization. Both
are so beautiful. I've decided that I'm NOT
going home!

53. Kaitlin: Range of Writing and Sketches from Field Trip to Aquarium (Jellyfish); Whale Watch; Hike ("Clover Bed" Poem); *One Child*; *The Giver*; and Mountain Hike ("Children of the Mountains" Poem)

Children of the Mountains
Kaitlin

Misty hills, lolling mountains,
Titans of the world, you lie;
in deep slumber.
We climb your sides, so that perhaps
  we can see all   you see.
Our feet grind the sand beneath us, while
We slog through dribbling streams.
I feel my heart beating at my chest
pounding-
  blood through my temples, to my legs.
Beating rythmically, like a chant:
go, go, go!
The intoxicating smells of the pines
  envelope me,
  and my spirit is free of its tired body.
We run across the beaten trail, and
reach the top. Enter the sky.
  We call ourselfs hikers.

54. Kaitlin: Range of Writing and Sketches from Field Trip to Aquarium (Jellyfish); Whale Watch; Hike ("Clover Bed" Poem); *One Child*; *The Giver*; and Mountain Hike ("Children of the Mountains" Poem)

Patrick

©2007 by Linda Rief from *Inside the Writer's-Reader's Notebook*. Portsmouth, NH: Heinemann.

2/10
Astronomy
30 min
2/11
Astronomy
30 min

The moon is 400 times smaller in diameter than the Sun, but it is 400 times closer to the Earth. Because of this, the Moon and the Sun occupy almost the same angle in the sky, ½ of a degree. This is why solar eclipses occur.

(I don't understand the connection? Can you explain it?)

2/12
Astronomy
1 hr 30 min

Tides are directly related to the gravitational pull of the Moon on the oceans of the Earth. It can be logically deduced that since gravity pulls stronger on closer objects. Water on the side of the Earth facing the Moon should be pulled away from the surface of the Earth, creating one high tide every day. However, two high tides occur daily. To explain this, I am going to draw a picture on the next page.

I can't stop reading this Cosmos book, because every page is filled with knowledge, and I love learning.

55. **Patrick:** Thoughts Stemming from *Astronomy*; the Holocaust; and *Cosmos*

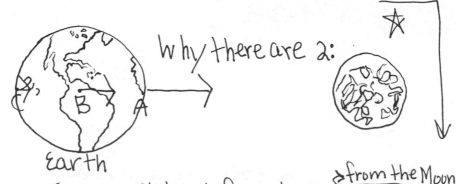

Why there are 2:

Earth

→ from the Moon

Since gravitational force lessens with distance there is more gravitational pull on point A than point B, and more on point B than point C.

One high tide is now at point A because the water there is being pulled with more force than the rest of the Earth, so it is being pulled relatively away from the Earth. The high tide on the other side of the Earth is ~~pulled~~ a result of the opposite effect. Since the pull at point B is stronger than the pull at point C, the Earth is being pulled relatively away from the water. The result of that is a higher water level relative to the Earth there as well.

As the Earth rotates, every point on its surface experiences two high tides. At the point B, and the point on the other side of the Earth equidistant to points A and C, there is a low tide. Therefore, every point on Earth experiences two high and two low tides every day.

56. Patrick: Thoughts Stemming from *Astronomy*; the Holocaust; and *Cosmos*

☆ On the subject of the Holocaust, I just remembered something that might be of intrest to you. I have some Nazi medals that my grandfather gave me from his service in the US Air Force in WWII. They look like this:

navy
red
navy
bronze(?)

I'm not exactly sure how he acquired these medals, but I could call him to ask. It's scary to think that these medals, which I am holding right now were once worn by a real Nazi. Not a Nazi from <u>Night</u>, a guard from <u>Schindler's List</u>, or a cartoon from <u>Maus</u>, but a real Nazi from Germany during WWII. He probably touched it right where I am now. Come to think of it, it was probably made by someone at a metal factory during the Holocaust, a Jew most likely.

He could have been from Night or Schindler's List. Those are real stories.

It is incredible that you have these. You must be curious about how he got them!

Yes, and that makes it especially sad!

57. Patrick: Thoughts Stemming from *Astronomy*; the Holocaust; and *Cosmos*

<u>Cosmos</u> Carl Sagan 11/12

"Between the orbits of Mars and Jupiter are countless asteroids, tiny terrestrial planets. ... The asteroid belt may be a place where a planet was once prevented from forming because of the gravitational tides of the giant nearby planet Jupiter, or it may be the shattered remains of a planet that blew itself up. This seems improbable because no scientist on Earth knows how a planet might blow itself up, which is probably just as well." This is a good quote because it combines lots of facts about the asteroid belt with the personal opinion that scientists can't be trusted with the knowledge of how to destroy Earth.

This book makes me think a lot about the universe. There is so much empty space out there. There must be laws governing this universe, but so few are known. Isaac Newton says "I do not know what I may appear to the world, but to myself I seem to have been only like a boy, playing on the seashore, and diverting myself in now and then finding a smoother pebble or a prettier shell than ordinary, while the great ocean of truth lay all undiscovered before me." This was about discovering the laws of the universe, of course.

I think I will write a piece based on what I've learned. It will be called <u>Collision</u> and be about a meteor heading towards Earth, and what everyone on Earth does about it.

58. Patrick: Thoughts Stemming from *Astronomy*; the Holocaust; and *Cosmos*

Laura

September 9

To be a good writer, you have to be alert.
You need to watch everything, you need to
observe with all of your senses how the ☆
world works. Watch people, watch trees and
rain and insects and cars. You need to breath
in what you feel and see, tumble it around
in your mind, and spill it out on paper.
    I don't know why I know that. That's
what writing is. Observing, feeling, than mixing
it all up in your head with what you
know and what you imagine.
        I write what's in my mind, and
I write from imagination, I think a lot.
I think out stories, and I'm always
observing everything I see, and trying to
anylize strangers. That's where my writing
comes from.
        The hardest part of writing for me
is bringing stories to a close. You couldn't
imagine how many bits and pieces of
stories I write, but I can't place
them and connect and resolve
them. let's try to do that!
        Oh - I forgot the easiest part. The
easiest part of writing for me is

© 2007 by Linda Rief from *Inside the Writer's-Reader's Notebook.* Portsmouth, NH: Heinemann.

59. Laura: "To Be a Good Writer . . ."; Reminiscing/Drafting Poetry About Her Grandmother; Response to *Of Mice and Men*

Student Notebook Samples ■ 1 0 5

writing in my head. It is so easy to make things come alive when they're trapped inside my mind, but when I attempt to make them paper-bound, they look useless.

I come up with ideas for writing by what I see and know and feel. These questions keep reminding me of Little Women, when Jo has to learn to write what she knows. That's true in some respects, but you shouldn't only write the truth, because with writing you have the opportunity to write anything — and you really ought to take advantage of that. So I write what I see, feel, and know, but also what I imagine.

Effective writing is alive, and it cages you in to it's own world.

I've never done a best piece of writing. I have so many tidbits of completley misc. writing, but I really wish I had a best piece.

I don't know what makes my writing better. When the muse strikes me,

60. Laura: "To Be a Good Writer . . ."; Reminiscing/Drafting Poetry About Her Grandmother; Response to *Of Mice and Men*

I write like mad, but when I'm in a negative mood, when every idea seems stupid, it's so difficult to write. I don't like it when everybody likes what I've written but me — but it happens that way.

☹ Last year, I would write for the grade — it was awful, and I never should have done it — but I felt forced to. I would write a few drafts, think it was perfect, and then I'd have a 'teacher conference', where I was basically told to "change the ending to your story or I'll mark you way down." What?!

My story at the time ended in a murder — NO! and the end was my favorite part — but I changed it just for the sake of getting a good grade, which was absolutley ridiculous. Now I hate the piece of writing. So, good effective conferences help my writing, but I do not like being forced to change things.

I like getting response but it needs to be honest, thorough, and advice. YES!

Why is it important to write well? Because writing is everywhere! Writing is in whatever career you follow. I'm kicking around several careers to follow in my head right now,

61. Laura: "To Be a Good Writer . . ."; Reminiscing/Drafting Poetry About Her Grandmother; Response to *Of Mice and Men*

a swingset. They form a little pretzel shape at the top where the knot is.

I found them in the bathroom closet when I was looking for bathtoys when I was little. Then they were lost for years and years collecting dust in the corner behind the sink, and then I found them again.

⭐ When my grandmother died, the world stopped. I didn't hear anything after "Your granny..." I just glared down at the kitchen table, and chewed off the skin on the inside of my cheeks and counted bread-crumbs. There were seven. In a little swept up pile on the kitchen table there were seven breadcrumbs. Seven. Seven crumbs had ~~fallen off~~ stumbled off someone's bread and onto the counter. Poor breadcrumbs. They would never have the chance to be eaten. They'd just be swept away into the garbage basket. All seven. One by one. I pitied the breadcrumbs. I swept them up in my hand and I started to

62. Laura: "To Be a Good Writer . . ."; Reminiscing/Drafting Poetry About Her Grandmother; Response to *Of Mice and Men*

eat them. One by one. They tasted
funny - like sponges. But I ate every
single one. They were tumbling around in
my mouth doing sumersaults. Why
were they so happy? Did they want to
be eaten? I guess they did. That's
when I spit out all the seven
breadcrumbs one by one into the
waste basket. All seven. One by one
I watched them shikt there
way down on the garbage roller
coaster to the endless pit of the trash basket
and I started to cry.

Oh... tell
me more
about your
grandmother!

   I don't know why I wrote
that, but it's true. I remember it
so well. Breadcrumbs. hmm...
   People are always asking me if
"Life's too short to drink cheap wine."
Personally, I think Life's too short
to ponder over that too much.
   Why am I scared of cities? Good Question
Actually, I like cities. Sometimes. They
have the potential to be very
interesting. So I can't say I'm completley
against them. You see, I'm kind of
scared of being murdered, but at

63. Laura: "To Be a Good Writer . . ."; Reminiscing/Drafting Poetry About Her Grandmother; Response to *Of Mice and Men*

Student Notebook Samples ■ 1 0 9

When my grandmother
died, all of her belongings were
sold, kept, or givin away. I got a sweater.
It isn't a very pretty sweater.
button up, cuffed sleevs, robins egg
blue - But the reason I got it
wasn't because of the way it looked
I got it because of its smell

It smells so much like my
granny it's like she's standing in
the room when I smell it.

I don't know how to describe
the smell - a rosey, canberry, buttery
smell - a wive smell. It's the smell
of running along the beach with
her tossing up breadcrumbs for the
seagulls. It's the smell of birthday
cards labeled "Love is Laura" that
always came on February 7th, one
day early. It's the smell of
christmas hugs and an extra
treat on Easter It's the
smell of riding a merrigo-
round with my granny
riding next to me

This is beautiful, Laura -
prose poetry. What a treasure
you have! I hope my grandchildren
will miss me this much!

64. Laura: "To Be a Good Writer . . ."; Reminiscing/Drafting Poetry About Her Grandmother; Response to Of Mice and Men

Of Mice and Men

Lennie is such a good character. He's so sincere, so honest to himself. I really love the relationship between George and Lennie.

It's interesting how Lennie likes animals so much, how it calms him to stroke them. What might this represent? I really have to keep reading. I'm almost done and I want to near the end! I'll be right back.

I HATE GEORGE! I HATE HIM! I hate Curley and I hate his wife and I hate Carlson and Candy and Slim. And I hate Lennie.

I don't understand this book at all. I'm in a state of shock and I can't figure it out. I can't. Why? Why so many things?

Why did George kill Lennie? Why didn't they run across the river- escape? Why did Lennie kill →

65. Laura: "To Be a Good Writer . . ."; Reminiscing/Drafting Poetry About Her Grandmother; Response to *Of Mice and Men*

Curley's wife? Did he do it on purpose? *I don't think so... OK*
But that's so much against every-
thing I believed about Lennie. And
George- I trusted George- I trusted
him to love Lennie and be his brother
Is that why he killed him? Why,
why, why! I don't know what
to think. What does it all mean?
What does all of this represent?
I just don't understand it. I've
laughed and cried through this book,
I've loved it and hated it and I
still don't understand. The end is
just so shocking -so unreal.
  I don't know what else to say.
Right now I'm feeling fear. Fear
towards the story- towards what the
metaphor is - and I'm feeling
hatred- for the characters -all over
again. I hate George, and Lennie
and Slim. I hate all of them.

  Laura, I think *Of Mice and Men* is a complicated
book. You are a sophisticated reader who understood
a lot and trusted George to care for Lennie. You cared
about Lennie. You read deeply, trying to figure
out and understand so much of what those relationships
were. I think Steinbeck forewarned us about Lennie
through the rabbits - he loved soft things but didn't
know his own strength. I think George loved him
like a brother + was afraid for him- the way others taunted
and mistreated him. I think he loved Lennie so much
he had to kill him, knowing others would do it because
they didn't know or care that what Lennie did was an accident.
                                        What do you think?

©2007 by Linda Rief from *Inside the Writer's-Reader's Notebook*. Portsmouth, NH: Heinemann.

66. Laura: "To Be a Good Writer . . ."; Reminiscing/Drafting Poetry About Her Grandmother; Response to *Of Mice and Men*

9/23
slam!
Walter Dean Myers
45 min.

9/24
slam!
35 min.

Andy

How is this different from your lifestyle?
What's life like in "the hood"?

slam is awesome. IT brings you to a new lifestyle, the hood.

Slam, or Greg, lives in the hood and has got game, in basketball. It's cool to read something that has words like "fly", "dig it", and "homey" in it.

Slam is having troubles in school though, especially math. It's got to be really frustrating, to not be able to even understand math. His friend Mtisha and a tutor have tried to help him but so far he hasn't responded to their efforts. I think this

Why do you think he hasn't responded?

is stupid of Slam because if he does not improve his grades he might be kicked off of the basketball team.

Slam's friend Ice seems to be getting involved with dealing drugs. The book portrays this as a common thing in the hood. Mtisha has told slam to talk to Ice about it but so far Slam has avoided the subject with Ice. This is stupid of Slam because he might end up seeing his friend in jail, which would not be fun, especially if you think that you could have done something about it.

67. Andy: Response to *Slam*; Thoughts on Boating

When slam has something
on his mind, it is on his mind.
Sometimes it's funny to see how
much slam thinks through simple
topics like going to Mtisha's house
to study.   *What makes this kind of thinking*
                                funny?

    Recently slam's brother Derek,
lost a video camera that slam
loned from the school. I know
what it feels like to lose something
important like that, and it doesn't
feel good. If slam doesn't
find   the camera, he will
probably have to replace it, and
his family ~~is not~~ doesn't have
much money. ~~The~~ It must be
a scary feeling.
    I love the basketball
parts in this book. Basketball
is slam's life and it is my
favorite sport so I can
relate to the things he feels
during basketball. He is really
good and it's fun to hear
about him slam dunking
and doing well in his games.

What's a passage about basketball
that you really like from this book?

What do you think Myers wanted readers to
take from Slam's life? What did you think
about him as a person?

68. Andy: Response to *Slam*; Thoughts on Boating

5/7

★ The waves lapped up
against the side of our boat
as it cut through the dark green
water. I turned the wheel over
to my dad and crawled along
the side of the boat, being
catious not to fall into the
cold water. When I reached
the mast I stood up and rested
against it, the cold penetrating
through my shirt and sucking
the heat from my spine. I looked
up. Beyond the sail, taut
with the saltey sea breeze that
powered our boat, the creamy
blue sky streched away in all directions
~~meeting the shores in~~ I looked
back and saw the serene green
waves, chopping into the calm afternoon.
Our boats white-green wake streched
out behind us, ending abruptly.

Beautiful images- prose- poetry!

*I certainly can see the pleasure
you take from sailing! Makes
me feel like I missed something special.*

©2007 by Linda Rief from Inside the Writer's-Reader's Notebook. Portsmouth, NH: Heinemann.

69. Andy: Response to *Slam*; Thoughts on Boating

Sarah J.

1|8

Just Another Kid
by Torey Hayden
6 1/2 hours   ✓

This book is very thought
provoking as many of Torey Hayden's
books are. I just couldn't put it
down. It also made me feel depressed
and guilty. So many times I feel bad
for myself because something
goes wrong like my dad loses his
temper and I flee to my room
crying, or I don't get the perfect
score on a test but there is so
much I have that others don't
have at all. Some of the kids
(and adults) in this book have
problems with speaking, hearing,
understanding, and much
more   things that I've never
had to deal with. I wish
that others just like I was only

thinking about themselves, would
read books like this.... and
experience guilt like I have. It really
helped me look at life in a different
perspective ....through someone else's
eyes.
                  Maybe "guilt" is not the way we
              should feel. Maybe more sensitive,
              more empathetic, more respectful
              of others.

©2007 by Linda Rief from *Inside the Writer's–Reader's Notebook*. Portsmouth, NH: Heinemann.

70. Sarah J: Response to *Just Another Kid*; *Night*; a Seminar; and *The Giver*

(✳)✳   2/13
     I would like to write a very
delayed response ~~tha~~ to Elie Wiesel's
book "Night". I've wanted to express
my feelings about it ever since I
finished the book but its so hard
to get in touch with my feelings. I
feel alone.... everyone else seems to
have come to terms with the
Holocaust. It happened ....its over....
all we can do now is look back
and read all the stories that
describe the horror and terror.
Its really hard for me to read
Elie Wiesel's book without
relating my life to it. what
would it be like? As I lie in bed at
night, staring at the ceiling, I try
feel the pain ... experience the
nightmare. But I can't. I see the
smoke, see everything, but I
can't feel anything.... I don't
know how to feel. I still don't
think that I have realized that
the Holocaust really took place.
It's hard - really hard. Night
really woke me up...shattered
the glass I was once surrounded
by. All that he has gone
through...losing all that really

©2007 by Linda Rief from *Inside the Writer's-Reader's Notebook*. Portsmouth, NH: Heinemann.

meant a lot to him, watching the world fall apart without being able to fight it, but most of all seeing his dreams turn to dust right before his eyes. Many times throughout reading the book I went so far as to throw the book across the room. I was so mad — but at whom? I was made at the Nazis, Hitler, all the hate but most of all— myself. How could I sit here and feel bad about myself for not living in the perfect world while I during the Holocaust people would do anything for a crumb-something to satisfy their hunger. What is wrong with me? I could feel the tears rolling down my cheeks- I couldn't stop them. I felt as though I was crying for everyone who lost something in the Holocaust -the poor babies whose lives were whisked away before they had a chance to live, the children who lost their families and forgot how to love, the Germans forced to take part in the nightmare that cast a

©2007 by Linda Rief from *Inside the Writer's-Reader's Notebook*. Portsmouth, NH: Heinemann.

72. Sarah J: Response to *Just Another Kid*; *Night*; a Seminar; and *The Giver*

giant shadow on their lives, and
I also wept for what our world
has become — a gathering of hate.

√ ✗ Its amazing how easy you can   2/14
lose everything in your life that's
really important to you. By making
the wrong decisions, your life can
really be shattered in the future. It's
really hard to pick up the pieces
of this shattered life and put
them back together again — and
start over. Because your past is
always there to haunt you.
          All these seminars were kind
of scary. Just the idea of choices.
Choices that will effect our lives.
Its hard to think about our
future — there's so much
unknown about it. A big
blank. It's really hard for me to
think about and imagine the
future when I don't even know
what to expect. Mrs. Roy said
"you enter your teenage years as
a piece of coal, and after
undergoing tremendous pressure
you emmerge as a diamond."
          😊 You have so many
          opportunities — that you
          will make the most of.

73. Sarah J: Response to *Just Another Kid*; *Night*; a Seminar; and *The Giver*

3/13
The Sunflower Forest
1 hour

3/14
The Giver
Lois Lowry

* Questions. Unknown. Wonder. The Giver is so thought provoking. This is probably because of how hard it is for me to grasp, to relate to Jonas' lifestyle. Though there are many similarities, their are also many differences and those differences are what stay with me. No feelings? How could they be so blind - not know how to love, to hurt, to feel pain? I know that it's not all the people's fault - that they were brought up this way - but still..... why? The part of the book which really made me cry (the first time I read it) was when Jonas watched the release. Death?!? The poor twin, not even a chance to live, proven unworthy of life because of weighing one pound

Actually, an ounce...!
Think of the irony - his father - the nurturer is the one who injects him! And the irony of precision of language and "release." Frightening world!

74. Sarah J: Response to *Just Another Kid*; *Night*; a Seminar; and *The Giver*

Tania

Tania, you have so many unique stories to tell about visiting your grandparents and other relatives in Bulgaria. Tell us more!

10/4

The Golden Compass
8:30 - 9:15

"Before she could go out on deck, the outer door opened and Ma Costa came down, swathed in an old tweed coat on which the damp had settled like a thousand tiny pearls."

I really liked the underlined description, I can imagine it clearly and it reminds me when my grandmother, in the early morning when I was waking up, would come in, wearing an old brown ✗ coat covered in dew from the cool morning. She would start making breakfast, and I would watch her, because in the summer it gets so hot that we have to sleep downstairs in the kitchen. The first night we wanted to try sleeping upstairs, but at around 2 in the morning, my sister, my cousin and I walk downstairs (this is an old house, so the stairs are on the outside

©2007 by Linda Rief from Inside the Writer's-Reader's Notebook. Portsmouth, NH: Heinemann.

75. Tania: Memories of Bulgaria in Response to *The Golden Compass*; *The Power of One*; Thoughts on Ethnic Albanians in Comparison with the Holocaust; Drafting Stories About Bulgaria

of the house) and knock for 5 minutes until my grandma wakes up and unlocks the door, then we have to put chairs on the edge of the bed so that we can all fit on the bed in the kitchen. With our legs resting on the chairs we fall asleep in the cool dark room.

After writing this I remember something else about sleeping in the kitchen. First of all I would like to mention that because the house is so old the kitchen is just a room with a dull wooden floor a bed, a table with mismatched chairs a few old cabinets and a wood stove, there isn't a sink or a normal electric stove. Any way, when we were sleeping downstairs, we would wake up every 2 hours to check if the cow was giving birth, and every time I got out of bed, I could feel the cold screaky floor until I find my slippers. Then I would tiptoe out to see how the cow was, and it was always fine. Finally on our last day on the farm she gave birth to a girl that I helped name "Maria".

However, I might not have seen the birth, because we had left to go the Black Sea, but after we were there for about six days, we called my grandparents and it turned out that the day that we had left, my grandma had been hit by a cow and was in the hospital, so we had to come back. She got better but she had had a broken rib and bruises.

76. Tania: Memories of Bulgaria in Response to *The Golden Compass*; *The Power of One*; Thoughts on Ethnic Albanians in Comparison with the Holocaust; Drafting Stories About Bulgaria

The Power of One
1:15-2:00

"Besides, I was beginning to understand how manipulation can be an important weapon in the armory of the small and weak."   pg. 42

The boy is very clever and smart and thinks. That can be a great advantage. The smarter people usually beat the strong people who don't think.

"One thing is certain in life. Just when things are going well, soon afterward they are certain to go wrong. It's just the way things are meant to be."   pg. 44

"I knew then that the person on the outside was only a shell, a presence to be seen and provoked. Inside was the real me, where my tears joined the tears of all the sad people to form the three waterfalls in the night country."   pg. 48

That's what the dream stood for. I don't know how he survived. All that torture, I could barely read about what they did to him. I think that it's so sad. And they were so young and had all that hatred. He didn't do anything wrong. He couldn't choose who he was going to be born, that he was born English. But even so, they are blaming what happened in concentration camps on him. It's just awful. Reading this book makes me sad, but I also feel hope for him.

©2007 by Linda Rief from Inside the Writer's-Reader's Notebook. Portsmouth, NH: Heinemann.

77. Tania: Memories of Bulgaria in Response to *The Golden Compass*; *The Power of One*; Thoughts on Ethnic Albanians in Comparison with the Holocaust; Drafting Stories About Bulgaria

whole world was destroyed what would happen? If the
After hundreds of thousands of years will new
species form, other people? Would history repeat
itself? It just makes me think of other questions
the we don't have answers for. Like where does
the universe end? It has to end somewhere
right? I've carried that same question with me for years!

   Getting back to the book, I think that it is
so creative how the title is related to it. Anne
always thought that Zachariah was the last
man. Kinda like how they are the last ones.
The last ones alive in the world probably.

                                                4/8
   To me, the way that the ethnic Albanians are
treated is like how the Jews were treated in the
Holocaust. Yeah they aren't being killed, well actually
they are. But even if there aren't any death camps,
they are forced out of their country and robbed
of what they believe. How can the Serbians be
calling NATO Nazis? Americas isn't killing a people
because of who they are. How can it be right to
do that? Why do people believe that it's right? Is it
greed? Are they greedy to have a nation of just
one race and religion? Do they think that its right
to force people out of the country because they
believe that it's not the Albanians' country? It's not

78. Tania: Memories of Bulgaria in Response to *The Golden Compass*; *The Power of One*; Thoughts on Ethnic Albanians in Comparison with the Holocaust; Drafting Stories About Bulgaria

their country, even though they were born there.

I wonder if the people of Serbia agree with Milosevic. They probably don't know what's happening in Kosovo. They don't get the whole picture because of the media filtering. I think that they also aren't on our side because they are being bombed. I see why we are bombing the military bases, but I don't see how it helps the situation. It makes the Serbians madder and it doesn't do anything for the Albanians.

Will this become a war? When and how will it end? Someone in the class said there will always be dictators. Is the power of power so great? Does it control the dictators?

"We are up against a dictator who has shown time and again that he would rather rule over rubble than not rule at all, someone who recognizes no limits on his behavior except those imposed by others," President Clinton said.

I am going to do an interview with my dad. He is a nuclear engineer and he helped build a nuclear power plant. I want to hear his opinions and along with the interview I want to write a paper on my opinions. *Great idea!*

Thoughtful questions!

R+
B½

---

79. Tania: Memories of Bulgaria in Response to *The Golden Compass*; *The Power of One*; Thoughts on Ethnic Albanians in Comparison with the Holocaust; Drafting Stories About Bulgaria

©2007 by Linda Rief from *Inside the Writer's-Reader's Notebook*. Portsmouth, NH: Heinemann.

~~Driving~~ the wagon   Nice!   ✓   (Name?)

"Dee, dee! Haide Koah!" Baba yells. The donkey bounces
up and down. Tic, tac, tic, tac.... The legs keep moving. How
can he keep going? The humid air surrounds everything and his
dark hair absorbs all of the sun's heat.
    The wagon is ~~all~~ full of bags. Heavy bags of grain
that ~~would~~ will be used to feed chickens and make bread.
    It seems so hard, up hill all the way back! Baba says that
he's a strong donkey and he can handle it. And when she feels
like he is going too slow, she slips her hand to the side of the
wagon. She pulls the whipping stick. She touches his back. He jumps
and tries to go faster, but the load is too big. Baba doesn't hit ✓
him again.
    She doesn't like using that whip, but she does. She's the only
one ~~that~~ who can. I jump off the wagon to ease the load. To make
his hard work easier.   You would do that ☺!

Driving
"On the way back to the farm we can take the black road,"
Baba says. That means I get to drive. I'm so bad, I can't
control the donkey because I don't want to hurt him or push him
too hard. And it's something new to me, unlike for Ana, who spends
her whole summer on the farm. what does the wagon look like? Where are you on it? Who is Ana? What are you doing?
    For me, driving the wagon is like when Todor learned to, drive the car.
We were coming back to the farm on the black dirt road. Dust   Who is Todor?
and smog building up in a cloud in the back, as we rumble through
the fields of corn and sunflowers! All is pretty good, until we
reach the end of the black road and switch to rocks.
    The town is ~~###~~ in a valley, and the roads on the hills leading from the
black road are made of rocks. Seeing that this was Todor's
first drive he was doing pretty well.
    We were four people in the back and Todor and my

©2007 by Linda Rief from Inside the Writer's-Reader's Notebook. Portsmouth, NH: Heinemann.

80. Tania: Memories of Bulgaria in Response to *The Golden Compass*; *The Power of One*; Thoughts on Ethnic Albanians in Comparison with the Holocaust; Drafting Stories About Bulgaria

uncle in the front. All of a sudden the car starts going faster. → Say this in Bulgarian.

"Stop!" Yells uncle Dancho.

~~Right then there is a turn.~~ In a quick reaction to that shout, Todor pushes ^down^ the gass pedal. The piece of red metal ~~came~~ ^comes^ alive and just as we ~~were going~~ ^are^ diving ^straight^ into a tree, Uncle jumps up and turns the wheel.

Branches stick through the open window. The air is still. Finally we ~~start to~~ breathe. A turn and a hill ago we were commenting on how ~~much~~ sick we were from the bobbing of the car because Todor couldn't change the gears. How we couldn't speak. → How did he try?

I think Baba or Uncle will start to ~~laugh~~ yell and get angry. But Baba just starts laughing and says, "Lele, was that close?!"

↗ Bulgarian then English!

Boustana

a town?

Today we are going to Boostana. We usually go to get a few watermelons or some cantelope, but today we are digging up potatoes. We'll stay there in the sun, digging up tiny brown potatoes. For lunch we'll eat some mellon and go back to filling bags. *How do you dig up potatoes?*

When I stop to rest I sit on the wagon and ~~look.~~ I look at the hills covered in fields and boostanas. I look at the trees ~~and~~ and their shade that covers the dried up river. I even look at the dead cow, hanging from a stick with a string attached to it wing. Swaying there to scare off the other birds. I look everywhere, with cool breeze drying up my sweat.

As the sun starts setting, we drive back with potatoes that ~~would~~ ^will^ hopefully last all winter. *where will they store them?*

81. Tania: Memories of Bulgaria in Response to *The Golden Compass*; *The Power of One*; Thoughts on Ethnic Albanians in Comparison with the Holocaust; Drafting Stories About Bulgaria

Freedom

Brian

A couple weeks earlier, we were each given a question regarding Freedom in Social Studies class. My table had been given the question "Should some ~~rights~~ rights be sacrificed for others?" My table responded "yes." However, I think that the question goes a lot deeper than a yes or no question, as there are exceptions and many situations when this ~~may~~ may not apply. For example, one gives up the freedom to kill in order to protect other citizens' rights to live. However, should one give up the freedom to privacy for the government's right to protect its nation?

Then there were the focus questions given throughout our revolutionary war project. Probably the most interesting one I've found was ~~probably~~ "What does it mean to be truly free?" Freedom is the state of being free from restraints. But really, the colonist fought for their independence, and for freedom. They had planted the seeds for our country, and our future. Unfortunately, many of our citizens can't ~~all even~~ take advantage of the freedom that the colonists fought so hard for. Gays don't have the freedom to wed, unwed/young woman might not be able to abort a baby that they aren't even prepared for, and many of us will no longer have the freedom of privacy because of the Patriot Act.

But that's beside the point. To be truly free is nearly impossible, even with democracy, revolutions, whatever. To be truly free can only be achieved through Anarchy, though common sense instantly tells us that even through anarchy the chances of you still being able to retain certain rights are slim to none, so there is no way to be truly free.

82. Brian: Just Thinking . . . About Freedom; the Poem "We Wear the Mask"; *The Journal of Joshua Loper*; Knowing History; Ignorance; Importance of Homework and Hard Work; the Poem "If We Must Die"; Internment Camps; and Homework Survey and Results

_12/14_

We Wear the Mask
By Paul Laurence Dunbar

So well said!
(TK)

   I have decided to choose this poem for my December poem because it is true to so
many people. The poem basically tells how in our society, we put on a false mask only to
hide our true feelings. We may act happy, but we may really be sad, or we may act tough,
but break down on the inside. It also enlightens those who are ignorant, helping them
realize what really goes on in other people's minds. It really makes you think about how
someone feels when you say different things. You may make a cruel joke towards a
friend, and on the outside they may try to laugh with you, but they might really be angry
on the inside. Things that you say always have an effect on the people you say them to, so
no matter what it is, you should always think about what you say before you say it.

	13/6/6	(13/6)+⁺ _I really enjoyed reading your question about "freedom"_
13/15	To Kill a Mockingbird	60 mins
12/16	To Kill a Mockingbird	90 mins

Brian, while I really enjoyed reading your response
to the question about freedom posed to you by
Mr. Nichols - (that made you pose even deeper and
wider questions to yourself - to be free we really
do have to adhere to certain rules and laws -
so can we be truly "free") - it took me awhile
to read your handwriting. I noticed you typed
your reasons for choosing each poem of the month
and found those _so_ easy to read.
     It would help me immensely if you
typed more of your responses to reading / thinking
about all you notice in the world. You have
so many provocative, insightful things to say -
I want to understand them and don't want
handwriting to get in the way. Thanks for considering this.

83. Brian: Just Thinking . . . About Freedom; the Poem "We Wear the Mask"; *The Journal of Joshua Loper*; Knowing History; Ignorance;
Importance of Homework and Hard Work; the Poem "If We Must Die"; Internment Camps; and Homework Survey and Results

1/27

<u>The Journal of Joshua Loper</u>

After I finished <u>Monster</u> for the author study, I moved on to reading <u>The Journal of Joshua Loper</u>, and I <u>must</u> say, I can't believe this <u>book came from the same author</u> of <u>Monster</u>. The <u>sentences are choppy</u>, the <u>verbs are vague</u> and could be <u>clarified, the characters have very little development and depth,</u> and it seems like Joshua <u>himself</u> is simply a two <u>dimensional character</u>. Now, this <u>whole thing could be</u> Myer's <u>way of using voice</u>, as this is the <u>journal of a teenage boy</u>, but seriously, I <u>haven't read a worse book since 5th grade</u>.

As I said before, the sentence structure used is very choppy and hardly ever gets to a point. For example: "Then he wrapped the roll in some muslin and boiled it. It was delicious and I was no longer the least bit mad at Isaiah. After dinner we sat around the campfire and had a good talk. Jake asked me to sing 'Just Before the Battle, Mother' again. Since I was not in such a bad mood as I had been before, I did." As you can see, every sentence within that excerpt could be compressed and combined into more useful sentences, saving time and space in the book.

If this really was a way to show Joshua's voice in his writing, then Walter Dean Myers has taken realistic fiction to a whole new level. If he chose to do his writing exactly like an uneducated boy would in the eighteen hundreds, he succeeded.

The characters also are very shallow, telling very little about each one, and hardly even telling anything about the "main" character. The <u>most you know about any other</u> character (Doom, in this case) is that he is <u>religious, he</u> <u>can shoot a gun</u>, he's <u>black</u>, and he's tough. That's all that is ever given, and <u>I for one, can't possibly bear to read a book without knowing who you're reading about</u>.

84. Brian: Just Thinking . . . About Freedom; the Poem "We Wear the Mask"; *The Journal of Joshua Loper*; Knowing History; Ignorance; Importance of Homework and Hard Work; the Poem "If We Must Die"; Internment Camps; and Homework Survey and Results

I don't know how commonly this is asked, but a couple of times I've heard some of my classmates complain about Social Studies class. Normally, this is just a normal complaint about homework or how annoying/monotonous it is, but also I've heard someone ask why they even need to know about what happened some 100 years ago. Now, this really irks at me. I mean, why SHOULDN'T we learn our past? That's practically the same as not wanting to know what you did for half your life, or what you did earlier today.

But also, someone once said that history is doomed to repeat itself. Obviously, if you don't know your past, how could you possibly prevent something from repeating itself? If a generation is raised off of the belief that history isn't important, what's there to stop another holocaust? Another 9/11? Another... Anything? I believe that it's amazing that we're able to be so intelligent, and that we're able to learn as quickly as we can. The sad thing is that so many people decide not to use anything they're given. They refuse to learn, and they'd rather sit on their butts all day. *Sad, but true!*

Now, I'm not trying to single anyone out, but this is one of the biggest things that annoy me. Ignorance. People act as if they'll be rewarded for not doing anything, and they only want to do the easiest things possible, get out of anything they can. But why? Because they'd rather watch TV and gossip with friends?

I just don't understand why people act this way. They might come from a less-fortunate family, but how do they expect to get a better life? Work hard. That's all you need to do to be successful in this world. Get an education and then get a good job. But what these people do is they don't try to do anything, and they figure "Hey, I'm not going to amount to anything, so why should I even bother?"

©2007 by Linda Rief from *Inside the Writer's-Reader's Notebook*. Portsmouth, NH: Heinemann.

85. Brian: Just Thinking . . . About Freedom; the Poem "We Wear the Mask"; *The Journal of Joshua Loper*; Knowing History; Ignorance; Importance of Homework and Hard Work; the Poem "If We Must Die"; Internment Camps; and Homework Survey and Results

There are a bunch of things that really irk me, but for the smaller things, there are a few too. One of those things is when people wind up calling me "Too smart", which is a huge overstatement in the first place. There is no such thing as Smart or Stupid in my book (at least, learning wise), since there are several things that make a person "Smart". You must be willing to learn otherwise you wouldn't be able to learn anything at all. It's like reading a good book. It's only good if YOU like it. You must be able to listen in class and when someone is helping you, since you can't learn if you don't listen. You've got to be willing to work for it. You can swallow a pill and instantly have 50 more IQ points. You have to work, as in studying a lot, doing all the homework, asking for help on subjects you don't understand, and know that it will all pay off in the end.

So really, all you need to do to get an A is listen, do homework, study, and understand the topics. Of all the above topics, I think that working hard is the most important. Like I said in an earlier entry, those who are getting F's are normally those who don't bother at all in class. Well, where do they go in life? Most likely they don't get too far. Why? Because they don't want to work. They won't get a good job, and even if

86. Brian: Just Thinking . . . About Freedom; the Poem "We Wear the Mask"; *The Journal of Joshua Loper*; Knowing History; Ignorance; Importance of Homework and Hard Work; the Poem "If We Must Die" Internment Camps;and Homework Survey and Results

they do they won't even bother trying at it. They won't get a good education, because

they don't want to do homework. Yet look at the people getting A's and high B's.

They're taking extra courses over the summer, learning a third language, applying to prep

schools, and all that. People complain that the smart kids always have everything coming

easy to them. Well guess what? They don't. Both the smart and the stupid take in

information at the same rate, but the smart people are the ones that know to retain that

knowledge, and the stupid are the ones who decide to throw it away.

I could not have said this more clearly! or succinctly!

3/11   February Poem (A little late…)
If We Must Die
By Claude McKay

(Brian has the poem written in his notebook.)

    I chose this poem as my February poem because I had been reading about

diseases in news articles, with all the treatments, all the side-effects, etc., as well as in

Life Skills we had been reading <u>Tuesdays with Morrie</u>. Mostly what I was thinking the

entire time I was reading them was "How could people possibly go through will all these

treatments, just to increase their lifespan by a year or so?"

    I mean, look at Chemotherapy for cancer. Each time you go to get that kind of

treatment, you get more tired and tired, the speed increased by the cancer itself. You lose

all your hair, and there's no real way to go out into public, because you're too weak to

even leave the house. But would this really be worth it all? I mean, you live a year more,

but what's the point? You're not even really living! Sitting in a bed at the hospital while

your friends and family come in to cry over you every day wouldn't seem like any way to

live, and I couldn't possibly fathom what it'd be like to be in that situation.

    But in Tuesdays with Morrie, Morrie uses his last few weeks to say goodbye to all

his friends and family, and he uses those weeks not to, but to teach. He doesn't waste his

time in bed crying about how life has treated him, and he "uses his time wisely" (as so

many teachers will have put it).

    But anyway, I guess it really does make sense. Within those few weeks, it could

be possible for a medical breakthrough, and there's always that slim hope for a miracle.

Like the poem says, don't go down without a fight.

87. Brian: Just Thinking . . . About Freedom; the Poem "We Wear the Mask"; *The Journal of Joshua Loper*; Knowing History; Ignorance; Importance of Homework and Hard Work; the Poem "If We Must Die" Internment Camps; and Homework Survey and Results

©2007 by Linda Rief from *Inside the Writer's-Reader's Notebook*. Portsmouth, NH: Heinemann.

3/23

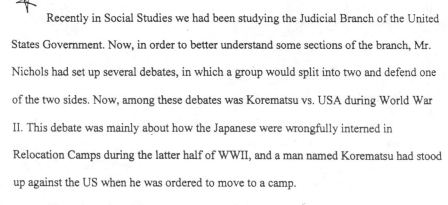

     Recently in Social Studies we had been studying the Judicial Branch of the United States Government. Now, in order to better understand some sections of the branch, Mr. Nichols had set up several debates, in which a group would split into two and defend one of the two sides. Now, among these debates was Korematsu vs. USA during World War II. This debate was mainly about how the Japanese were wrongfully interned in Relocation Camps during the latter half of WWII, and a man named Korematsu had stood up against the US when he was ordered to move to a camp.

     Now, the point of these camps was to defend the country itself from Treason, in case a Japanese citizen decided to defect to the Japanese forces and reveal all of our secret plans and objectives. So basically, the <u>main factor in creating the internment camps</u> was to protect the country. Later on, about 20 years after the war had ended, the Supreme Court had ruled that the interment camps were unconstitutional and had given every prisoner of the internment camps $20,000 in reparation money.

     Now let's look to the present. After 9/11, Bush had started his crusade against Terrorism, and the "axis of evil" in the Middle East. He had also decided to pass the Patriot Act, which <u>directly compromised our personal freedom for the sake of defending the country against terrorists within our country.</u> Take a gander at exactly why the Patriot Act had been passed, because we were afraid of Treason. Now let's look at why the Interment Camps were created, because we were afraid of Treason. <u>Both events had breached our rights as citizens and both are completely unconstitutional.</u>

     Now although the internment camps were on a higher scale, who's to say that the Patriot Act won't be escalated to the point where any possible threat will be thrown in prison, regardless of evidence? Both cases will turn out to be extremely similar, and yet many people have yet to realize it.

88. Brian: Just Thinking . . . About Freedom; the Poem "We Wear the Mask"; *The Journal of Joshua Loper*; Knowing History; Ignorance; Importance of Homework and Hard Work; the Poem "If We Must Die" Internment Camps; and Homework Survey and Results

If another terrorist attack occurs, I have no doubt that the nation will be in so

much turmoil that Bush will pass an amendment on the Patriot Act doing exactly as I said

above. Funny though, since no one seems to realize how similar the two cases are,

bringing me way back to knowing your history, and learning from the past. But that's

pretty much self-explanatory.

4/6

You know, I find it kind of funny at how the kids in the 8th grade choose to

express their arguments. Namely, the argument against the amount of homework we've

been getting. Now, don't get me wrong, I don't like wasting my time on worksheets or

workbooks when I could very well be watching TV or just laying around, but jeez! The

kids in my grade act like we get 17 worksheets a night with 3 hours of required reading!

At the start of Algebra class the other day, it was basically an open conversation about

how large the workload was per night, and Ms. Ellsworth took a poll of how long we

spent on homework per class. So we went through the classes, and the results basically

looked like this: Math – 45 Minutes

Foreign Language – 20-30 Minutes

Social Studies – 2 Hours

Language Arts – 1 Hour

Science – 1 ½ Hour

Now, take into account that this is the Algebra class, which is basically filled with

the more intelligent and over-achieving students (just a generalization). It shouldn't take

ANYBODY 2 hours to finish the 4 worksheets a night from social studies, and if it does,

you obviously have trouble working. I mean, it shouldn't take more than 5 minutes to

skim over a small reading section and answer 1 sentence questions. Math could take

about 45 minutes, so that's fine. Foreign Language assigns very little, so I agree with that

as well. Language arts is a bit exaggerated, since most people simply wait until something

89. Brian: Just Thinking . . . About Freedom; the Poem "We Wear the Mask"; *The Journal of Joshua Loper*; Knowing History; Ignorance; Importance of Homework and Hard Work; the Poem "If We Must Die" Internment Camps;and Homework Survey and Results

is due the next day to do it, and then complain about how long they had to work on it.

Then science I can partially agree with because of the recent major experiment, but in the

past week we've gotten little more than a worksheet every other day.

we're supposed to learn so that we are prepared for the future. I mean, Mr. Nichols makes

it a point to show us that we are the future, and that we have to be ready for whatever

comes our way. But I've ranted enough, and it's late.

Post note: As I mentioned, it's late, so there are probably a lot of grammatical errors.

Also, please don't mention this to any of the other teachers during a meeting or anything.

Just my blatant ranting here. *Not to worry! It's important ranting that makes me think!*

Brian, tell me what works in your classes. Where are you learning? and in what ways is that learning able to happen?

9/13/10

I won't mention it!

H(t) Impressive! What do you think as you read 1984?

9/14

Brian, I've been thinking about all you said in here for the entire day. I went back and looked through your entire journal. It's amazing how often you talk about things you've learned in social studies. I'm also impressed with how much more thoughtfully you approach books, writing, issues... Looking back often surprises us— The more I look at your writing, the more I understand + recognize how deeply you are thinking!

90. Brian: Just Thinking . . . About Freedom; the Poem "We Wear the Mask"; *The Journal of Joshua Loper*; Knowing History; Ignorance; Importance of Homework and Hard Work; the Poem "If We Must Die" Internment Camps; and Homework Survey and Results

Je

Dawn <Favorite poems of Emily Dickinson>
                                    By; Emily Dickinson

When night is almost done,
And sunrise grows so near
That we can touch the spaces,
It's time to smooth the hair.

And get the dimples ready,
And wonder we could care
For that old faded midnight
That frightened but an hour.

What makes this one of your favorite poems?

11/29

Tuck Everlasting (c1, c2),
(3:00~4:30)   a read
                                    By; Natalie Babbitt
   I decide to write two chapters a day, because
each chapters are very short. Anyway, I read
this book before in korea, so it will help me
to understand perfectly. ~~It stat~~ This story starts
with image of the village(3) the story starts.
Most important thing is that there are
~~two~~ forest named Treegap and I think
it is the main place of this story.
Then ~~the~~ this story tells about characters.
in each chapter. Tuck's are people who lives.
in the forest, and they are going to meet ?
their sons in ten years. ~~A~~I think Mae wm'
who is wife of Tuck, is very good mother.
~~sh~~She will go to the village ~~to meet~~

91. Je: "Dawn," Response to *Tuck Everlasting*; American Jokes; *Daniel's Story*; *Freak the Mighty*; Thoughts on "Afraid"; "English"; Thoughts on *To Life*

Student Notebook Samples ■ 1 3 7

their boys little earlier. Tuck is very
good (I think), but he is little lazy. He
don't want to go out. At this point I
have got a question. When Mae was leaving, she
said to Tuck to be careful. Then Tuck said
"What in the world could possibly happen to me?"
Is he a god? He have to be careful. I
think there are some secret in ~~His~~ his
talking. I'll see...
loved part: I loved part it said that
'Nothing ever seems interesting when it
belong to you - only when it doesn't.'
Because I agree at this scentence.
I always feel that. If my brother
got something, ~~than~~ I always wanted
to have that. Even a small toy.

11/29

'time flies'
'Time flies'. This means that time is going
fast than usual. I feel that, too. Especially
in U.S.A. After I came to U.S.A, time goes
~~more~~ faster than ever. I think I came here
3 months ago, but already. 6months passed.
It is almost December now. ~~If~~ I think this
way, it is not ~~too~~ so long to stay in U.S.A.
I am going back to Korea on next ~~J~~July,
so I want to know more about English.
My English is not clear. Sometimes I am thinking
that I don't want to go back to Korea.

91. Je: "Dawn," Response to *Tuck Everlasting*; American Jokes; *Daniel's Story*; *Freak the Mighty*; Thoughts on "Afraid"; "English"; Thoughts on
To Life

But, korea is my country. I have to go back.
I hope Time goes ~~very~~ more slowly. Now I can
understand ~~so's me~~ the korean saying 'Time
is ~~so~~ gold'. When I was young, I felt
silliness ~~on~~ at this scentence, but now I can
understand it. I should ~~study~~ study and learn
about English ~~more~~ harder.

You are doing very well!
11/30

Tuck Everlasting (c3, c4)
(3:45 ~ 4:30)   By: Natalie Babbitt
Chapter 3 and 4 ~~were~~ still talking about characters.
Winnie Foster is 10 years old girl who ~~don't~~ doesn't
like her life, because of their family. Their
family alway keep their eyes on her. ~~It~~ means
they love Winnie a lot, but she doesn't like
that. I can understand. Sometimes, people
wants to be alone. She is talking to toad
about her feeling. (silly.) She said, 'I will, though.
You'll see. Maybe even first thing tomorrow, while
everyone's asleep.' ~~Will she~~ Is she going to
run out from her house? ~~a~~ Anyway another
character is a stranger. People never met him,
but he is being kind to everyone. Who
is him? Is he bad side or good side?
I hope bad. I think Tuck's ~~are~~ seems
kind and friendly and Winnie is young, so
if this stranger is bad side, the story
will be more interesting.

92. Je: "Dawn," Response to *Tuck Everlasting*; American Jokes; *Daniel's Story*; *Freak the Mighty*; Thoughts on "Afraid"; "English"; Thoughts on *To Life*

©2007 by Linda Rief from *Inside the Writer's–Reader's Notebook*. Portsmouth, NH: Heinemann.

Tuck Everlasting (c5)   12/01
(4:00~4:30)   By: Natalie Babbitt
   At last, she went out from her house while
family are sleeping. Actually, she was just taking
a walk at the forest. Then she met a
boy. I think she felt very good at him.
His name is Jesse Tuck. He is one kid of
Tuck's. Now ~~they~~ two main characters met.
Something will happen now. Anyway, Winnie
want some water, but Jesse doesn't ~~give~~ give
her water, though he has one bottle of water.
He is acting weird, when Winnie asked him
for some water. Is there any secret in
that water? While Jesse was having
a trouble with Winnie, Mae ~~come~~ and
his another son come to them. When
they ~~are~~were coming Mae said strange
words. 'Well, boys, here it is. The worst is
happening at last' What is the worst?
I can't imagine.

                                       12/01
funny jokes?
   I can't understand American jokes. Sometimes
teacher said a joke, ~~the~~ then everyone
laugh. Except me. I am feeling 'What's so
funny?' I can understand what does he talking,
but I can't understand the funny part.
I always think 'How can that be funny??'

93. Je: "Dawn," Response to *Tuck Everlasting*; American Jokes; *Daniel's Story*; *Freak the Mighty*; Thoughts on "Afraid"; "English"; Thoughts on *To Life*

in trouble. I want to say this first.
Sometimes I feel really bad in school.
Some kids think I am Chinese or Japanese.
I know that Korea is not that usual to
American people, but there are one country
~~is~~ named ~~Korea~~ and Koreans are using a
Korean. ~~People~~ should never think Koreans are
using Chinese or Japanese. ~~Peole~~ People will
understand ~~man~~ me when they hear same
thing like me. I feel really bad when
they are asking me about Japanese and
ask me to read it. I have no idea how to
read that Japanese. Anyway, I hope
people to not to think I am Chinese or
Japanese. Sometimes Americans
           are not very thoughtful!
                                    12/04

   Tuck Everlasting (c9)
(기억이 안나서45)
                             By: Natalie Babbitt.
   Now ~~stus~~ Winnie met Tuck. Tuck is very
surprised at her. It was very good to him
to see the person who is living normaly.
I felt little sorry for them. If they
lived like this, it means they don't
have any friends to play with or talk
with. Poor people. It will be very boring
and sad, if there is no one to be
a friend. Every friends will think strange,
if they meet Tuck's. They didn't
changed at all.

94. Je: "Dawn," Response to *Tuck Everlasting*; American Jokes; *Daniel's Story*; *Freak the Mighty*; Thoughts on "Afraid"; "English"; Thoughts on
To Life

<Daniel's story>

"If I had the power of God, I would wipe the entire human race off the face of the earth. It's a complete failure. Look ~~to~~ around us, a race of monsters."

This passage shows how terrible ~~looks~~ ~~to~~ people looked. ~~the~~ They are thinking they are monsters. They ~~are~~ are thinking this way by themselves. ~~to~~ When I saw the picture of Jews, I felt really ~~sorry~~ sorry. They were too thin. They were almost skeletone. How can they stand up? If they ~~didn't~~ look at the mirror, they won't recognize who it is. Even though it is their face, they will scream by horror. How terrible. Now I can understand, why did people tried to die. They didn't wanted to feel ~~more bad~~ worse things. They thought it will get worse to live. If I was living in that time perioud, I would cry for a day. Maybe, for a week or more. ~~to~~ I can feel sadness by reading a story. Then, how sad will it be to live. It's just horrible

02/18

95. Je: "Dawn," Response to *Tuck Everlasting*; American Jokes; *Daniel's Story*; *Freak the Mighty*; Thoughts on "Afraid"; "English"; Thoughts on *To Life*

So, the toad is going to live forever. But, does he know that he is going to live forever? Anyway, why did Winnie gave up ~~the~~ everlasting life? Was she afraid of being alone? But, she has Tuck's, if she drink the water. It ~~will~~ would be hard to choose. Now there are one more chapter left. Actually, it is epilogue. What is left? This story is ende! ~~But~~ I will read epilogue slowly, than any other chapters, so I can have a fun at last.

Would you want to have everlasting life? Why? or why not?
                                                                    12/19

Freak the mighty
~~I~~ I think this story is wonderful. It showed a great friendship, and what is life. The death of Kevin made me little ~~sad~~ sad. I felt sorry when Max hit the glass with his hand and yelling. It was kind of adventure and dramatic story. Max will hard to forget Kevin, Kevin was the big part of Max's life. But I think Kevin will always alive in Max's heart, and head. We can say Kevin gave a courage to Max, that he ~~&~~ can write something as others. I can't explain everything, but I have many feelings. I ~~think~~ hope people should read this story, and have some great feelings.

©2007 by Linda Rief from Inside the Writer's-Reader's Notebook. Portsmouth, NH: Heinemann.

96. Je: "Dawn," Response to Tuck Everlasting; American Jokes; Daniel's Story; Freak the Mighty; Thoughts on "Afraid"; "English"; Thoughts on To Life

97. Je: "Dawn," Response to *Tuck Everlasting*; American Jokes; *Daniel's Story*; *Freak the Mighty*; Thoughts on "Afraid"; "English"; Thoughts on *To Life*

"Prose—words in their best order; poetry—
the best words in their best order"
                    Samuel Coleridge, 1835

_____

                                    03/13

✶ Afraid
    Sometimes I feel really funny about my
mind. Whenever I am thinking about Korea,
I'm kind of afraid about it. I think
it's because of korean school. The way
they teach is different with here, Maybe,
I'm afraid about going back to korea. What
if no one remembers me? What if they
know a lot more than me? This feeling
is the thing that I felt, right before
I came to America. Afraid of new world?
Korea is my country, but I've been here
too long(?), so that I can't even remember
the place I lived. Sometimes I feel bad
about my parents, because they took
me here. But this one year gave me
an experience of living in
another country. In my mind, afraid and
happiness are mixed up together.
        It's always frightening to live somewhere
            that's so different! But-it is so rewarding!

©2007 by Linda Rief from *Inside the Writer's-Reader's Notebook*. Portsmouth, NH: Heinemann.

98. Je: "Dawn," Response to *Tuck Everlasting*; American Jokes; *Daniel's Story*; *Freak the Mighty*; Thoughts on "Afraid"; "English"; Thoughts on *To Life*

English.

Sometimes I really don't understand English and American people. How can Americans possibly remember everything about English? I mean there are so many things to remember in English, such as ~~an~~ articles, idioms and other things. It ~~can~~ can be hard for me, because I'm not American, but I learned English from a long time ago. But, ~~is~~ it's still hard for me to put articles, such as `a`, `an`, `the`. I'm kind of having a ~~$~~ problem with articles, but others are using ~~to~~ those easily. When ~~I am~~ (me and) my friends and are working in the ESL class, Mrs. Garvey usually makes us ~~to~~ correct other kid's' writings, but sometime I can't find any. ~~them~~ Others find tons of wrong vocabularies from other's writings. That makes me kind of sad. It reminds me how ~~I am~~ dull Not at all I am. ~~I think~~ I'm doing my best, but I guess it's not enough. ~~An Any we~~ Anyway, it will take ~~forever~~ to learn the perfect English.

Ask all the Americans here to speak Korean. See how hard that would be for them — then you'll realize how much you know!

99. Je: "Dawn," Response to *Tuck Everlasting*; American Jokes; *Daniel's Story*; *Freak the Mighty*; Thoughts on "Afraid"; "English"; Thoughts on *To Life*

146 ■ INSIDE THE WRITER'S–READER'S NOTEBOOK

03/31

To Life (c7)
(7:30 ~ 8:00)   By: Ruth Minsky Sender

   I think I like this writer's writing style. This book describes well about people's feeling. Sadness, when the people couldn't find their family. Joy, when they found their family or remind themself that they are not in the Concentration Camp anymore. Anyway, I found one interesting thing. Actually, it is an interesting question. Is this story a real story? ~~In this book~~ ~~#~~ The name of the main character in this story is Riva Minsky, and the name of the author of this book is Ruth Minsky Sender. Since people put the name of their ancester as a middle name, I thought that this author could be a ~~g~~grand daughter or a daughter of Riva Minsky. Maybe, this author made up this person with using her name. _This is her true story!_

04/01

To Life (c8, c9)
(7:00 ~ 7:30)   By: Ruth Minsky Sender

   I think ~~#~~ writing a response to this book is such a hard job. I can enjoy and feel lots of things while I'm reading, but I can't describe those feelings with my

©2007 by Linda Rief from Inside the Writer's-Reader's Notebook. Portsmouth, NH: Heinemann.

100. Je: "Dawn," Response to _Tuck Everlasting_; American Jokes; _Daniel's Story_; _Freak the Mighty_; Thoughts on "Afraid"; "English"; Thoughts on _To Life_

Own words. I can't think of the best word to describe the feelings. Even I tried, it kind of doesn't make any sense. ~~By~~ But, I'll keep try ~~s~~ to describe it. Anyway,

★ I felt as if I was reading <u>Romeo and Juliet</u> in this chapter. <u>Riva and Moniek met and married together almost right away.</u> Even they felt lonely and even they felt love to each other, how ~~could~~ can they marry each other ~~s~~ in that ~~short~~ time? Marrying is not a thing to choose right away. I personally think that marrying is a ~~start of a~~ beginning of a big trouble. Some poets and writers said that marrying is a begining of an adventure. But, that's just ~~for~~ Romeo and Juliet. We are not Romeo or ~~Juliet~~ Juliet. Think of how easy people get divorced and remarry⁎ in these days. In Romeo and Juliet's time period, if one person ~~is~~ married with ^{another} ~~one~~ person, they had to live together forever. But in ~~te~~ these days, marrying is kind of same as buffet. Try this person, and that person. I don't know how this writing became like this, but my point is that <u>Riva and Moniek should have ~~this~~ thought of their marriage ~~for more~~ ^{for} longer time.</u>

Do you think they might have felt they didn't have much time?

©2007 by Linda Rief from *Inside the Writer's-Reader's Notebook*. Portsmouth, NH: Heinemann.

101. Je: "Dawn," Response to *Tuck Everlasting*; American Jokes; *Daniel's Story*; *Freak the Mighty*; Thoughts on "Afraid"; "English"; Thoughts on *To Life*

These must be "moon pebbles" lining the shore; with each wave the rocks wash over each other, the sound of rain sticks from the rainforest, tumbling their way back to the ocean floor. Cool breeze washes over my back, despite the hot sun. I love that sound of Atlantic Ocean, pulling on the rocky shore. "Come with me, come with me," she says. White foam waves - rocks over rocks over rocks - clattering - chattering... The sounds of the natural world are so much more appealing to me than man-made - waves slapping on a rocky shore, the cardinal-bright red sitting in our peach tree - with his high-pitched trill - 3 sharp shreeks -- everyone walks by hardly glancing at the ocean or her waves or her powerful arms sweeping rocks back home - people, they are in a hurry - on their way to find purple T-shirts, postcards of the ocean - caught forever in silent tide - or rum raisin ice cream, salt water taffy, lobster rolls - without ever a thought to the burly-armed, deep-bronzed men who heft the heavy lobster pots from the ocean floor while their boats bob back and forth with each deep sigh of the ocean - I love that rattle of rocks. I'd love a house on top of a cliff in Maine, where I could fall asleep each night to the sound of wave against rocks

Mrs. Rief

July 8
Perkins Cove, ME
Hunter's 4th Birthda

Edward Hopper said: "If you can paint rocks, you can paint anything!"

Sitting on rocks leading to Marginal Way!

E.H. may be right - this is HARD!

©2007 by Linda Rief from *Inside the Writer's-Reader's Notebook*. Portsmouth, NH: Heinemann.

102. Mrs. Rief: Field Trip to Perkins Cove; Notes on Teaching; Storyboarding "Eleven;" Quickwrites/Watching Grandkids; Response to *Nothing But the Truth* and Notes from Kids "What's Keeping You Reading?"; Watching My Students Watch *Anne Frank,* the Movie; Notes from NCTE; Drawing Ayera and Jack as They Read; Response to *My Sister's Keeper*; Field Trip to JFK Library; Listening and Watching Reactions to *Anne Frank;* Converence Notes, Speaker David Carroll; Anita Shreve at the Bookstore; Notes from Island Trip; Teaching a Course in Vancouver, WA; Note/Response to Mike

Sept. 3rd   O RMS

Marcia Ross- principal- quoting Alvin Toffler - "The illiterate of the 21st Century will not be those who cannot read and write, but those who cannot <u>learn</u>, <u>unlearn</u>, and <u>relearn</u>! "

1st day- cut up 5 pieces of poetry- "The Summer Day" Oliver
           "The Writer"- Wilbur
           "Eighth Grader"- Thomas (use w/ adults -kids don't find funny!)
           " Growing Up" K. Wilson
           "Autumn"- Pastan

Had kids find the pieces that went together - arrange in order-
read int end - I talked about each as related to class. Next
time: ⌐all poems same font so they must read for topic + languag.
     | add a humorous one
     | make sure each has a distinct voice or rhythm
     └(different fonts made it too easy!)
     kids talked to each other to find pieces and order

2nd day - had kids choose, organize journals

Should have been the smooth, typed notebook. not coil

→NAME - SECT.
→ LMR   1st page- cardboard
→ NOTES   divider- ½ way thru journal
→ VOCAB.   20 pages from spelling page
→ SP.   3 pages from back

Reading List - Expectations   stapled onto 1st (cardboard) page

3rd day -   Sept. 6
     Love That Dog   } 1st entry
     Sharon Creech
     30 min.

Just listen- may draw as I read- related to what you hear-
how does Jack change from beginning to end?
How does that happen?

on overhead- put up Jack's poem - "My Sky"- that he typed himself -
     quickwrite - all/anything brought to mind
         - choose a line - write off line
         - draw - from any image that came to mind

103. Mrs. Rief: Field Trip to Perkins Cove; Notes on Teaching; Storyboarding "Eleven;" Quickwrites/Watching Grandkids; Response to *Nothing But the Truth* and Notes from Kids "What's Keeping You Reading?"; Watching My Students Watch *Anne Frank,* the Movie; Notes from NCTE; Drawing Ayera and Jack as They Read; Response to *My Sister's Keeper*; Field Trip to JFK Library; Listening and Watching Reactions to *Anne Frank;* Converence Notes, Speaker David Carroll; Anita Shreve at the Bookstore; Notes from Island Trip; Teaching a Course in Vancouver, WA; Note/Response to Mike

Spencer- "You know how I know where the west is? The terrorists always say 'We are going to bomb the west!' That's us -so I know we're the west!"

Sept. 8, '03 was Hunter's 1st day of kindergarten - riding the bus has been a terrible experience - he has sobbed before getting onto the bus, and broken into tears after getting off the bus - one day Jennifer had to carry him onto the bus, him screaming, holding onto her legs - Jennifer crying as the bus pulled away -

Storyboard as Retelling

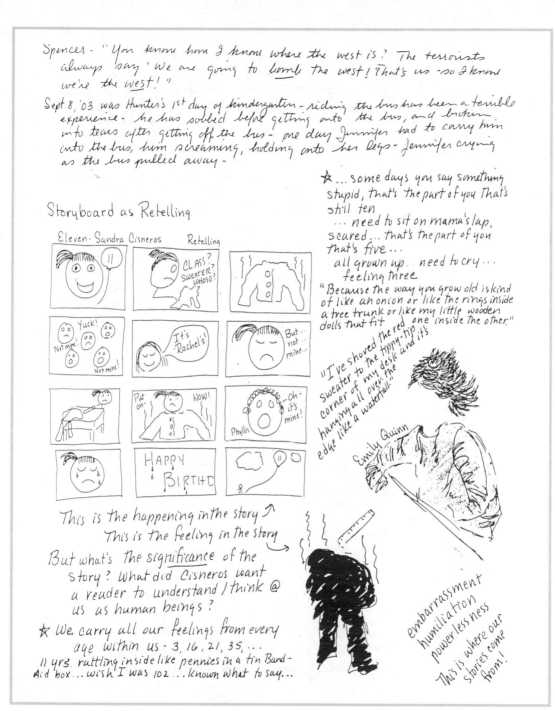

Eleven · Sandra Cisneros   Retelling

☆ ...some days you say something stupid, that's the part of you That's still ten
...need to sit on mama's lap, scared... that's the part of you that's five...
all grown up.. need to cry... feeling three
"Because the way you grow old is kind of like an onion or like the rings inside a tree trunk or like my little wooden dolls that fit one inside the other."

"I've shoved the red sweater to the tippy-tip corner of my desk and it's hanging all over the edge like a waterfall!"

Emily Quinn

This is the happening in the story ↗
This is the feeling in the story

But what's the significance of the story? What did Cisneros want a reader to understand I think @ us as human beings?

☆ We carry all our feelings from every age within us - 3, 16, 21, 35, ...
11 yrs. rattling inside like pennies in a tin Band-Aid box ...wish I was 102 ...known what to say...

embarrassment
humiliation
powerlessness
This is where our stories come from!

104. Mrs. Rief: Field Trip to Perkins Cove; Notes on Teaching; Storyboarding "Eleven;" Quickwrites/Watching Grandkids; Response to *Nothing But the Truth* and Notes from Kids "What's Keeping You Reading?"; Watching My Students Watch *Anne Frank,* the Movie; Notes from NCTE; Drawing Ayera and Jack as They Read; Response to *My Sister's Keeper*; Field Trip to JFK Library; Listening and Watching Reactions to *Anne Frank;* Converence Notes, Speaker David Carroll; Anita Shreve at the Bookstore; Notes from Island Trip; Teaching a Course in Vancouver, WA; Note/Response to Mike

I wrote: I never thought I felt anything for animals but on the day that Amish, our first Doberman, tangled with a porcupine and had quills sticking from her nose, inside her mouth, her cheek, her whole face, I felt so bad for her - I knew she was crying with the pain - and it made me cry looking at these large black-saucer eyes filled with tears and pleading "help me help me help me..."   OR

⟶ This line makes me think of Grammy Mac, that day I found her in the nursing home, fingers encrusted with dry food, an overflowing catheter bag,... whispering "her, help me help me"   OR

borrowing a line - I was playing with Hunter when he was 9 mos. old, holding his tiny hand as he tried to climb a stack of books in his room and I turned around and when I looked back he was 4 yrs. old sitting on his bed surrounded with books, opening up How Does a Dinosaur Say Goodnight and saying "Read this one, Grammy!"

(Talked about how one piece of writing leads to others!)
    in LA Sect. 4   Kelvin, Emily, Sam - wonderful quickwrites

Fri. after school - to Winecellar to see H+H - played with them in field - we broke off cat-tails, climbed a big rock, and used them as fishing poles - "Oh. oh ..." says Hunter, as the pole shakes + pulls in his hand "I got a feisty one ..." and he reels him in + flops him into the boat. Harrison does the same, then flings his pole into the water "Oh, no"... "he took my pole..." And Hunter climbs down, ~~wrestles~~ the fish, and gets Harrison's pole. "Tanks," he says.
    wrestles

Thurs. after school I babysat Julia - she now (7 mos. old) gets up on her knees and crawls - she loves toys she touches that flash + make music - I took her in the stroller for 20 min., we played on the floor (I built the legos, she knocked them down), fed her milk/bottle (she fell sound asleep in my arms curled up like a little teddy bear against me), awoke, fed her jar of chicken/squash. She loved it. ate all. then a bath + 'jamies - all clean when daddy came home - also brought her several outfits from Gymboree - so cute - hooded jacket... knit long sleeve one piece...

©2007 by Linda Rief from Inside the Writer's-Reader's Notebook. Portsmouth, NH: Heinemann.

105. Mrs. Rief: Field Trip to Perkins Cove; Notes on Teaching; Storyboarding "Eleven;" Quickwrites/Watching Grandkids; Response to *Nothing But the Truth* and Notes from Kids "What's Keeping You Reading?"; Watching My Students Watch *Anne Frank,* the Movie; Notes from NCTE; Drawing Ayera and Jack as They Read; Response to *My Sister's Keeper*; Field Trip to JFK Library; Listening and Watching Reactions to *Anne Frank;* Converence Notes, Speaker David Carroll; Anita Shreve at the Bookstore; Notes from Island Trip; Teaching a Course in Vancouver, WA; Note/Response to Mike

I want to respond to *Nothing But the Truth* by Avi.

I think Avi should have named this book EVERYTHING BUT the Truth! It seems to be more than a book about miscommunication – everybody acts in less than admirable ways and nobody is telling real truths. They seem to tell different truths to different people. Philip says he doesn't like his teacher before even arriving in her classroom; the teacher yells @ Philip in a rather pre-emptive manner, before he's done anything. She says the board wants her ~~forced~~ to resign when all they really do is ask her to take the rest of the year off – with pay! The supt. doesn't even know her, although he describes her as one of the best teachers in the district. And the parents – the father's angry at the world – (esp. his boss) – he never talks to anyone – the school, the teacher, his son – even jumps the gun with a politician on a local committee. I wonder what Avi wanted readers to get from this? What part of it was he writing for himself? To me the book is about listening / not listening – real lack of communication – reminds me – believe none of what you hear, only half of what you see! Whole book left me thinking – does anyone really care about the truth? The characters all seem exaggerated + self-protective – is that what SATIRE is – exaggeration of flaws – i.e. the idiocy of high school politics?

Kathy Cooper I asked – what's keeping you reading your book...?

Uncle Tom's Cabin

I choose to read Uncle Tom's Cabin because I read ~~Gone~~ With the Wind which said that slavery wasn't ~~to~~ bad and Uncle Tom's Cabin is about how bad slavery is.

Because Uncle Tom's Cabin was written while slavery existed it is very realistic and it's interesting how the author presents the fact that slavery is wrong with a story, but she also tells the reader.

Rose- A Girl Named Disaster
"... needed a book... mom says any award book is one of the best. I don't always think so."

Brian - The Amber Spyglass
"read two books from same trilogy... look forward to reading this. hope for great conclusion"

Anne of Green Gables   Angela Gong

I'm rereading this book because I have read the rest of the series, and I thought this book was the best. Anne is not nearly so annoying now as when I was 10. I keep reading because I remember things that happened, ~~So~~ and I want to read them again. Also, It's satisfying just to read.

Lacey: The Royal Diaries - Nzingha
"I love royal histories..."

Sam: Tantras
"... lot of action... plot detailed... fighting scenes good..."

Tim: Patriot Games
"saw the movie... liked it... so read the book."

Tom: Maus
"... want to learn more about how Hitler became powerful... and it's a cartoon..."

Zoe: Against the Storm "... takes place in Turkey

©2007 by Linda Rief from *Inside the Writer's-Reader's Notebook*. Portsmouth, NH: Heinemann.

---

106. Mrs. Rief: Field Trip to Perkins Cove; Notes on Teaching; Storyboarding "Eleven;" Quickwrites/Watching Grandkids; Response to *Nothing But the Truth* and Notes from Kids "What's Keeping You Reading?"; Watching My Students Watch *Anne Frank,* the Movie; Notes from NCTE; Drawing Ayera and Jack as They Read; Response to *My Sister's Keeper*; Field Trip to JFK Library; Listening and Watching Reactions to *Anne Frank*; Converence Notes, Speaker David Carroll; Anita Shreve at the Bookstore; Notes from Island Trip; Teaching a Course in Vancouver, WA; Note/Response to Mike

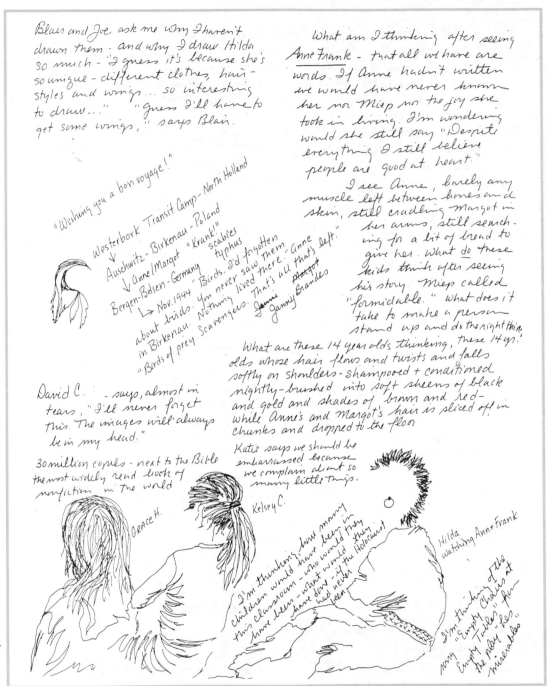

Blair and Joe ask me why I haven't drawn them - and why I draw Hilda so much - "I guess it's because she's so unique - different clothes, hair-styles and wings... so interesting to draw..." "Guess I'll have to get some wings," says Blair.

What am I thinking after seeing Anne Frank - that all we have are words. If Anne hadn't written we would have never known her nor Miep nor the joy she took in living. I'm wondering would she still say "Despite everything I still believe people are good at heart."

I see Anne, barely any muscle left between bones and skin, still cradling Margot in her arms, still search-ing for a bit of bread to give her. What do these kids think after seeing her story. Miep called "formidable." What does it take to make a person stand up and do the right thing.

"Wishing you a bon voyage!"

Westerbork Transit Camp - North Holland
↓
Auschwitz - Birkenau - Poland
↓ "Krank!"
Anne/Margot scabies
Bergen-Belsen - Germany typhus
↳ Nov. 1944 "Birds. I'd forgotten about birds. I've never saw them in Birkenau. Nothing lived there." "Anne's left." That's all that's left. Margot
Jenni Jenny Brandes
"Birds of prey. Scavengers.

What are these 14 year olds thinking, these 14 yr. olds whose hair flows and twists and falls softly on shoulders - shampooed + conditioned nightly - brushed into soft sheens of black and gold and shades of brown and red - while Anne's and Margot's hair is sliced off in chunks and dropped to the floor

David C. - says, almost in tears, "I'll never forget this. The images will always be in my head."

30 million copies - next to the Bible the most widely read book of nonfiction in the world

Katie says we should be embarrassed because we complain about so many little things.

Grace H.

Kelsey C.

I'm thinking, how many children would have been in this classroom - who would they have been - what would they have done - if the Holocaust had never been.

Hilda watching Anne Frank

I'm thinking of the "Empty chairs at Empty Tables" from the play "Les Miserables."

107. Mrs. Rief: Field Trip to Perkins Cove; Notes on Teaching; Storyboarding "Eleven;" Quickwrites/Watching Grandkids; Response to *Nothing But the Truth* and Notes from Kids "What's Keeping You Reading?"; Watching My Students Watch *Anne Frank,* the Movie; Notes from NCTE; Drawing Ayera and Jack as They Read; Response to *My Sister's Keeper*; Field Trip to JFK Library; Listening and Watching Reactions to *Anne Frank;* Converence Notes, Speaker David Carroll; Anita Shreve at the Bookstore; Notes from Island Trip; Teaching a Course in Vancouver, WA; Note/Response to Mike

Margaret Edson
 Wit = Pulitzer Prize
(worked in an AIDS/cancer unit in '80s)
- our struggle to live is our most
   important endeavor
- speech is alive - always NOW
- text is dead - when I write
   something down, it has left
   my body
- we are brought together by talk
- Socrates was a talker
- Plato was a writer

"My kindergarteners are
ruined by literacy. They
come in alive + full + rich."
"I resolve my conflict @
writing, by writing for theater."
"The play is meant to be heard,
happening to your body."
(How do we ever get into print
all those things going on at the
same time? ... the great glory
in the text is the silent part...
the print of a text should be to
get people to look up from the
text.)
"There must be something
greater that happens in the
classroom that is far greater
than the texts. It is ourselves - as people."

Nancy Johnson - keep in mind @ written response:
goal - for reader to interact w/ text
must be taught - modeled
see + hear good examples (collect lang./passages)
LR resp = powerful assessment tool
what if I put bookmark down one side of
page + show kids exact responses?

Purpose of extending
reading thru the arts
is to extend one's
developing understand-
ing - to pause - step
back:
What does this book
give you pause to con-
sider?

ART
How does project show what
I've learned?
When someone views my project, what will they learn about the book?

November 20

Dear Linda,

   As the holidays begin, I thought you might enjoy another touch of the mountains. It won't break; Hunter can take it down and hold it. May it remind you of how I treasure our friendship. I hope someday you and George can come see this part of the country.

   It was such a treat for me to spend time with you in Milwaukee. I especially enjoyed meeting Marcia. I told Richard the p...o...n...d... story today; he all but fell out of his chair laughing. I can't wait to share that one with our language arts department.

   Here's hoping the season will bring some quiet moments before the fire with a book and a glass of wine. The best part of the weekend at NCTE might have been our talk on the bus. Thank you for telling me how it is. I know of no higher compliment.

Lovingly,
Vivian

"I've come to a frightening conclusion that I am the decisive element in the classroom. It's my personal approach that creates the climate. It's my daily mood that makes the weather. As a teacher I possess a tremendous power to make a child's life miserable or joyous. I can be a tool of torture or an instrument of inspiration. I can humiliate or humor, hurt or heal. In all situations, it is my response that decides whether a crisis will be escalated or de-escalated and a child humanized or de-humanized."

Haim Ginott

©2007 by Linda Rief from Inside the Writer's-Reader's Notebook. Portsmouth, NH: Heinemann.

---

108. Mrs. Rief: Field Trip to Perkins Cove; Notes on Teaching; Storyboarding "Eleven;" Quickwrites/Watching Grandkids; Response to *Nothing But the Truth* and Notes from Kids "What's Keeping You Reading?"; Watching My Students Watch *Anne Frank,* the Movie; Notes from NCTE; Drawing Ayera and Jack as They Read; Response to *My Sister's Keeper*; Field Trip to JFK Library; Listening and Watching Reactions to *Anne Frank;* Converence Notes, Speaker David Carroll; Anita Shreve at the Bookstore; Notes from Island Trip; Teaching a Course in Vancouver, WA; Note/Response to Mike

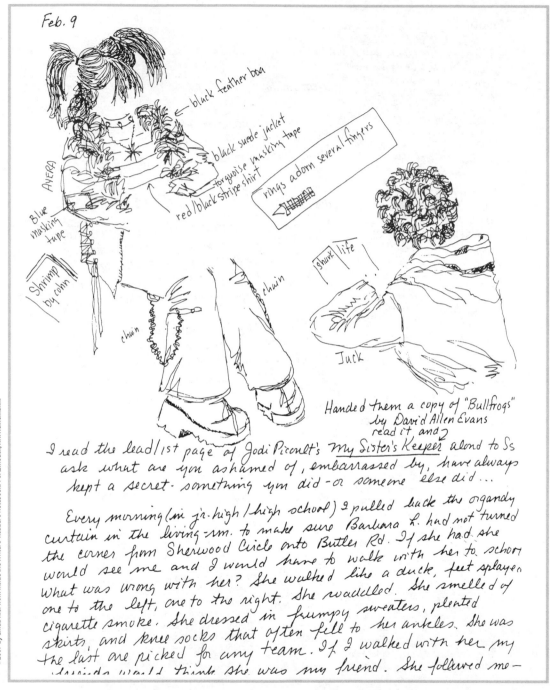

Feb. 9

black feather boa

black suede jacket

turquoise masking tape

rings adorn several fingers

red/black stripe shirt

AYERA

Blue masking tape

Shrimp by cohn

chain

chain

shark life

Juck

Handed them a copy of "Bullfrogs" by David Allen Evans — read it and

I read the lead/1st page of Jodi Picoult's *My Sister's Keeper* aloud to Ss — ask what are you ashamed of, embarrassed by, have always kept a secret · something you did — or someone else did...

Every morning (in jr. high/high school) I pulled back the organdy curtain in the living-rm. to make sure Barbara L. had not turned the corner from Sherwood Circle onto Butler Rd. If she had she would see me and I would have to walk with her to school. What was wrong with her? She walked like a duck, feet splayed one to the left, one to the right. She waddled. She smelled of cigarette smoke. She dressed in frumpy sweaters, pleated skirts, and knee socks that often fell to her ankles. She was the last one picked for any team. If I walked with her my friends would think she was my friend. She followed me —

109. Mrs. Rief: Field Trip to Perkins Cove; Notes on Teaching; Storyboarding "Eleven;" Quickwrites/Watching Grandkids; Response to *Nothing But the Truth* and Notes from Kids "What's Keeping You Reading?"; Watching My Students Watch *Anne Frank,* the Movie; Notes from NCTE; Drawing Ayera and Jack as They Read; Response to *My Sister's Keeper*; Field Trip to JFK Library; Listening and Watching Reactions to *Anne Frank;* Converence Notes, Speaker David Carroll; Anita Shreve at the Bookstore; Notes from Island Trip; Teaching a Course in Vancouver, WA; Note/Response to Mike

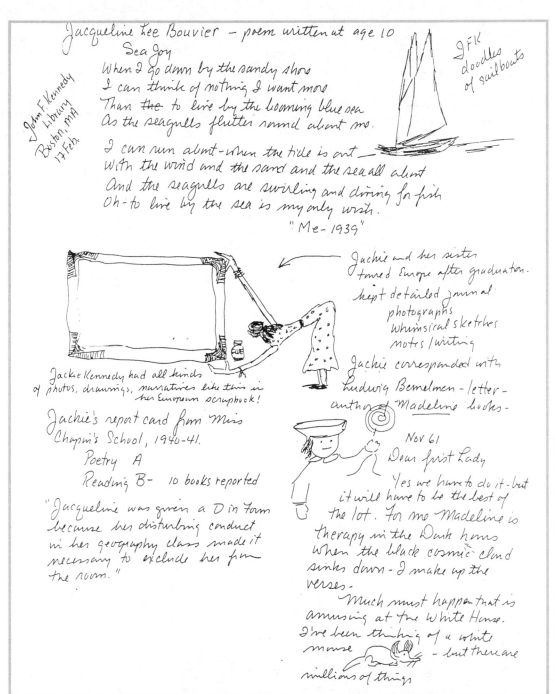

Jacqueline Lee Bouvier — poem written at age 10

Sea Joy

When I go down by the sandy shore
I can think of nothing I want more
Than the to live by the booming blue sea
As the seagulls flutter round about me.

I can run about - when the tide is out
With the wind and the sand and the sea all about
And the seagulls are swirling and diving for fish
Oh - to live by the sea is my only wish.

"Me - 1939"

John F. Kennedy
Library
Boston, MA
17 Feb.

JFK
doodles
of sailboats

Jackie Kennedy had all kinds
of photos, drawings, narratives like this in
her European scrapbook!

Jackie and her sister
toured Europe after graduation.

kept detailed journal:
photographs
whimsical sketches
notes/writing

Jackie corresponded with
Ludwig Bemelmen - letter -
author of "Madeline books -

Jackie's report card from Miss
Chapin's School, 1940-41.

Poetry   A
Reading B-   10 books reported

"Jacqueline was given a D in Form
because her disturbing conduct
in her geography class made it
necessary to exclude her from
the room."

Nov 61
Dear First Lady
          Yes we have to do it - but
it will have to be the best of
the lot. For me Madeline is
therapy in the Dark hours
when the black cosmic cloud
sinks down - I make up the
verses.
          Much must happen that is
amusing at the White House.
I've been thinking of a white
mouse   - but there are
millions of things

110. Mrs. Rief: Field Trip to Perkins Cove; Notes on Teaching; Storyboarding "Eleven;" Quickwrites/Watching Grandkids; Response to *Nothing But the Truth* and Notes from Kids "What's Keeping You Reading?"; Watching My Students Watch *Anne Frank,* the Movie; Notes from NCTE; Drawing Ayera and Jack as They Read; Response to *My Sister's Keeper*; Field Trip to JFK Library; Listening and Watching Reactions to *Anne Frank;* Converence Notes, Speaker David Carroll; Anita Shreve at the Bookstore; Notes from Island Trip; Teaching a Course in Vancouver, WA; Note/Response to Mike

May 22nd

★ Anne Frank — The movie with Ben Kingsley.

Hannah asks — "Why are they so cruel?" What makes human beings behave so cruelly to each other? Not just the Nazis. I can't understand how anyone believes they have the right — no — the desire to "exterminate" someone. How can that be? I cannot imagine the atrocities committed to other people — even today — children SOLD to rug makers in Pakistan and India — ? — I wish I had the courage, the tenacity of Ron Adams, whose 7th grade students have built 2 schools in Iqbal's name. What makes one person persevere — another just do the minimum. How bad can existence be when a pair of socks is such a gift?

Used Dave's "A Hollow Smile"
" Ann's "Simple Truths"

"That movie was very realistic, and crawled inside me and it's going to make me think and remember this forever. It's also sad that some of them died just a couple of days before the camps were liberated. Anne thought that her dad was dead. I wonder if Anne had known her dad was still alive, then she might have lived." David Curtis May 23 journal entry

Next year, stop to read diary entries of Anne's as we watch the film.

Pieces of writing to finish for end of year:
- hair - coupled w/ these pictures
- "Truth is" - coupled w/ pict. of Hilda
- tidal pool / beach piece

"One man with courage makes a majority." Andrew Jackson

Otto Frank: "Nothing makes sense ~~to me~~ anymore, Mr. Pfeffer, not to me... not anymore!... As long as my family can stay together."

Anne: A-25063

Watching Anne Frank

Hannah S.

Amelia C.

Emily T.

Emily J.

Alison K.

Jess

111. Mrs. Rief: Field Trip to Perkins Cove; Notes on Teaching; Storyboarding "Eleven;" Quickwrites/Watching Grandkids; Response to *Nothing But the Truth* and Notes from Kids "What's Keeping You Reading?"; Watching My Students Watch *Anne Frank,* the Movie; Notes from NCTE; Drawing Ayera and Jack as They Read; Response to *My Sister's Keeper*; Field Trip to JFK Library; Listening and Watching Reactions to *Anne Frank;* Converence Notes, Speaker David Carroll; Anita Shreve at the Bookstore; Notes from Island Trip; Teaching a Course in Vancouver, WA; Note/Response to Mike

"We are hard-wired to draw and tell, not to write!"

"Art professors said, 'This is an interesting idea!' First time anyone told me I had an idea!"

"They roll in a visiting author, and out crawls the Trojan Horse dyslexic."

"No test knows who the smartest kids are."

"Every McNeil-Lehrer news broadcast is storyboarded."

David Carroll -
has been following the trail of the spotted turtle since he was 8 yrs. old
(June 10th, 1950!)

TURTLES - 260 million yrs. old

No matter how many times I try to draw David, he still looks like Santa Claus! (not for real, in my sketch!)

WHITE-GOLD HAIR-BEARD
BLACK HEADBAND
RED SHIRT

Thoreau's Walden his real mentor

"What's a summer... consider the turtle." Thoreau

"I cannot think without a pencil."

"I write all my manuscripts + drafts in longhand."

Are kids losing the natural world -?- that's another reason to have kids keep nature journals - observe, stare, understand that the world is not plastic!

"Have you ever eaten turtle soup?" Someone asks.

"No!"... "Nor frogs' legs or salamander pie!"

Alice Walker: "If you write, you're a writer!"

"My workroom is so bad I'm almost paralyzed in it. I lay a board on top of work - then another board - when time dig thru two layers.... I need a taller stool."
What am I getting from this man? He is passionate about turtles, swamps, ... but he is not a very good speaker. This is disjointed, unorganized, not very helpful nor very interesting information. Why can men get away with talks like this?

"Zen-like state ... standing in solitude..."

Roger - cont.
in movie is high concept

Each sq. could be an idea - or a sentence.
Telling board = script for speaking

Writing comes from wanting to tell a story, not from being told to tell a story.
Law school - use storyboards to memorize @ case!

---

112. Mrs. Rief: Field Trip to Perkins Cove; Notes on Teaching; Storyboarding "Eleven;" Quickwrites/Watching Grandkids; Response to *Nothing But the Truth* and Notes from Kids "What's Keeping You Reading?"; Watching My Students Watch *Anne Frank,* the Movie; Notes from NCTE; Drawing Ayera and Jack as They Read; Response to *My Sister's Keeper*; Field Trip to JFK Library; Listening and Watching Reactions to *Anne Frank;* Converence Notes, Speaker David Carroll; Anita Shreve at the Bookstore; Notes from Island Trip; Teaching a Course in Vancouver, WA; Note/Response to Mike

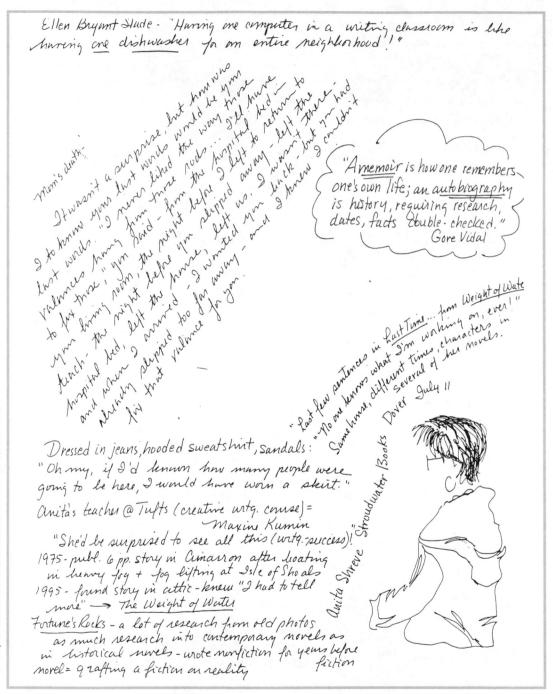

Ellen Bryant Stade - "Having one computer in a writing classroom is like having one dishwasher for an entire neighborhood!!"

Mom's death -

It wasn't a surprise, but those who
I to know your last words would be your
last words. "I never liked the way those
valances hung from those rods ... I'll have
to fix those," you said - from the hospital bed - to
your living room, the night before I left to return to
teach - the night before you slipped away - left the
hospital bed, left the house, left us. I wasn't there - had
and when I arrived - I wanted you back - but you had
already slipped too far away - and I knew I couldn't
fix that violence for you.

"A memoir is how one remembers
one's own life; an autobiography
is history, requiring research,
dates, facts double-checked."
Gore Vidal

"Last few sentences in Last Time ... from Weight of Water
"No one knows what I'm working on, ever!"
Same house, different times, characters in
several of her novels.

Anita Shreve Stroudwater Books Dover July 11

Dressed in jeans, hooded sweatshirt, sandals:
"Oh my, if I'd known how many people were
going to be here, I would have worn a skirt."
Anita's teacher @ Tufts (creative wrtg. course) =
                    Maxine Kumin
"She'd be surprised to see all this (wrtg. success)!
1975 - publ. 6 pp. story in Cimarron after boating
in heavy fog + fog lifting at Isle of Shoals
1995 - found story in attic - knew "I had to tell
more" → The Weight of Water
Fortune's Rocks - a lot of research from old photos
   as much research into contemporary novels as
in historical novels - wrote nonfiction for years before
novel = grafting a fiction on reality   fiction

113. Mrs. Rief: Field Trip to Perkins Cove; Notes on Teaching; Storyboarding "Eleven;" Quickwrites/Watching Grandkids; Response to *Nothing But the Truth* and Notes from Kids "What's Keeping You Reading?"; Watching My Students Watch *Anne Frank,* the Movie; Notes from NCTE; Drawing Ayera and Jack as They Read; Response to *My Sister's Keeper*; Field Trip to JFK Library; Listening and Watching Reactions to *Anne Frank;* Converence Notes, Speaker David Carroll; Anita Shreve at the Bookstore; Notes from Island Trip; Teaching a Course in Vancouver, WA; Note/Response to Mike

It is now 5:22 am. I've been awake all night. Migraine - took Fiorinal - did nothing - Imitrex tab - nothing - Imitrex injection - migraine subdued - still - no sleep - Tylenol PM - nothing - the rain is coming in on waves of wind - it is getting light - still - _no_ sleep - _none_ - why? want my own bed - my own sheets -

← Here's what I learned on that 2 hour trip across the sand "roads" twisting and turning and bouncing between scrub pine and marsh grass. I love the smell of salt water and seaweed and hip roses. I love the feel of salt spray on my face and the wild wind off the ocean brushing my hair. I love open spaces, where other people aren't allowed to go so that cormorants and eider ducks and loons and hawks and seagulls still know they own this space - they are not so afraid yet cautious enough to be a little weary. Yet, they have not learned of man's greed and selfishness and arrogance and carelessness. I learned I don't know enough to ask questions, especially of those things I wonder about.

What is that red spot on a seagull's beak?
Why do cormorants so often stand at the edge of water, wings spread wide to dry?
What's the difference between a mallard and an eider duck?
Why have I never seen a loon out of the water, on land?
How long does a yearling keep its spots? (a "yearling" perhaps)
How have those 2 stone chimneys stood tall and solid, battered by hurricane force winds, salt air and seawater, the roasting sun - while the houses around them crumbled and disappeared?

So amazing to me - fireplace chimney still as solid as the day it was built hundreds of years ago!

foundation of house crumbling - will undermine structure of chimney

To me this chimney is a symbol of the entire refuge; when we do the right thing to preserve a natural wonder, the area does flourish - birds, shrubs, fish, deer - even freshwater in the midst of brackish + ocean. This refuge is pristine, breathtaking because man has not been allowed to ruin it.

114. Mrs. Rief: Field Trip to Perkins Cove; Notes on Teaching; Storyboarding "Eleven;" Quickwrites/Watching Grandkids; Response to *Nothing But the Truth* and Notes from Kids "What's Keeping You Reading?"; Watching My Students Watch *Anne Frank,* the Movie; Notes from NCTE; Drawing Ayera and Jack as They Read; Response to *My Sister's Keeper*; Field Trip to JFK Library; Listening and Watching Reactions to *Anne Frank;* Converence Notes, Speaker David Carroll; Anita Shreve at the Bookstore; Notes from Island Trip; Teaching a Course in Vancouver, WA; Note/Response to Mike

©2007 by Linda Rief from *Inside the Writer's-Reader's Notebook.* Portsmouth, NH: Heinemann.

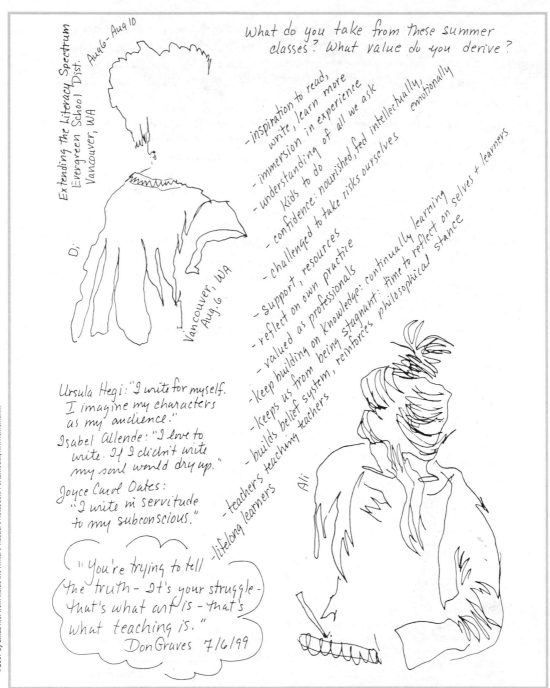

Extending the Literacy Spectrum
Evergreen School Dist.
Vancouver, WA
Aug 6–Aug 10

D.
Vancouver, WA
Aug. 6

What do you take from these summer classes? What value do you derive?

- inspiration to read, write, learn more
- immersion in experience
- understanding of all we ask kids to do
- confidence: nourished, fed intellectually, emotionally
- challenged to take risks ourselves
- support, resources
- reflect on own practice
- valued as professionals
- keep building on knowledge: continually learning
- keeps us from being stagnant: time to reflect on selves + learners
- builds belief system, reinforces philosophical stance
- teachers teaching teachers
- lifelong learners

Ursula Hegi: "I write for myself. I imagine my characters as my audience."

Isabel Allende: "I love to write. If I didn't write my soul would dry up."

Joyce Carol Oates: "I write in servitude to my subconscious."

"You're trying to tell the truth – It's your struggle – that's what art is – that's what teaching is."
Don Graves 7/6/99

Ali

115. Mrs. Rief: Field Trip to Perkins Cove; Notes on Teaching; Storyboarding "Eleven;" Quickwrites/Watching Grandkids; Response to *Nothing But the Truth* and Notes from Kids "What's Keeping You Reading?"; Watching My Students Watch *Anne Frank,* the Movie; Notes from NCTE; Drawing Ayera and Jack as They Read; Response to *My Sister's Keeper*; Field Trip to JFK Library; Listening and Watching Reactions to *Anne Frank;* Converence Notes, Speaker David Carroll; Anita Shreve at the Bookstore; Notes from Island Trip; Teaching a Course in Vancouver, WA; Note/Response to Mike

Mrs. Rief—
read this
when you can—
I'll be back

M. Zist /

p.s.— listening to the tape?
want more? Read the book!
(the whole thing, though)

Sept. 3   Mike Z. died yesterday—biking home from school—first day
Sophomore year—hit by a truck. I cried in class today. Mike was my
student in 7th grade—an awkward, gawky kid who had a hard time making
friends. Found friends in his reading—created friends thru his writing
He visited me often thru 8th and 9th grade. Brought me writing to
respond to—books he wanted me to love—all fantasy. I don't enjoy
fantasy—but Mike persisted. Just before school got out last June
he brought me a tape—Piers Anthony's The Magic of Xanth.
     "Listen," said Mike. "I figured it out. If you listen to
this tape while you're sleeping, I think you'll learn to like
these books. Sorta like learning foreign languages."
     I laughed—and promised again to read—and to listen.
Today I look around my classroom. Mike's books sit
gathering dust on top of my file cabinet. The tape? In
my desk drawer with broken pencils, pen caps, white-out,
and chess pieces. Michael's voice fills my room—in his
writing—in his books—his tape. I listened over the
years, but somehow I never really heard him.
     Now it's too late to let Mike know I cared enough to
try to like fantasy, for him. I read Mike's writing and cry
again. How many pieces like "Arthur" have I read—have
other students listened to—yet never really heard the writer's
voice? Tonight I'll listen to The Magic of Xanth.

116. Mrs. Rief: Field Trip to Perkins Cove; Notes on Teaching; Storyboarding "Eleven;" Quickwrites/Watching Grandkids; Response to *Nothing But the Truth* and Notes from Kids "What's Keeping You Reading?"; Watching My Students Watch *Anne Frank,* the Movie; Notes from NCTE; Drawing Ayera and Jack as They Read; Response to *My Sister's Keeper*; Field Trip to JFK Library; Listening and Watching Reactions to *Anne Frank;* Converence Notes, Speaker David Carroll; Anita Shreve at the Bookstore; Notes from Island Trip; Teaching a Course in Vancouver, WA; Note/Response to Mike

Afterword

As I was writing this guide I received an email from Lil, a former eighth grader, now a junior in high school. I hadn't heard from her in two years. What she had to say is important enough to let it stand by itself.

Wednesday, January 17 9:51 p.m.

Mrs. Rief, I counted my journals tonight. I have written 21 since eighth grade. Thank you!

Sincerely, Lil

Thursday, January 18 7:00 a.m.

Lil, it is so nice to hear from you. I am writing a book about Writer's-Reader's Notebooks and was wondering if you'd mind giving me a bit more information about these journals. What kind of writing/drawing do you do in them? What do you find most valuable about having these now?

Mrs. Rief

Sunday, February 25 10:34 p.m.

Subject: JOURNALS!

I would describe my journals as if they were a part of who I am. Their pages are like a record book of my life. The pages are not solely personal. They reflect on current events, a random person sitting across from me on the train, or how flustered I feel with all my responsibilities. Sometimes my journals become my mediator, allowing the pen to withdraw angry thoughts or a crushed heart. Other times it becomes a discussion board for important decisions.

 I have written numerous entries which should be entitled "Why I Write." I have not come to a solid conclusion. I have noticed that journaling calms me. Just a phrase can erase an entire week of tension. A page might smooth over a disagreement and propose an apology. My journal acts as a peer, yet one without judgment. It is always ready to listen, no matter how early in the morning it is. Somehow, and I haven't quite figured it out yet, journaling is rational. When I write about decisions I have made, I analyze them. The next time a similar situation arises, I will perhaps have an improvement to make. The endless hours I spend gives me the opportunity to tear apart who I am and what I want to become. Many are unable to grant minutes in order to scratch the surface of their complicated layers.

My father, though [he] never has discouraged my writing, is fascinated with the amounts of time I spend with a pen in my hand. It puzzles me too each time I sit down to write. No one has read my journals since you, in my eighth grade year. I would not permit anyone to read them if they inquired, for I discover things when I write. I notice things, which I would not have noticed otherwise. I dig deep into my thoughts and memories for juicy and interesting information, more than the gossip of everyday conversation. Sometimes I dive deeper and longer than I am willing to share with anyone other than my lined paper.

I read two books over vacation. Although they were both school assignments, I did not write one phrase about either in my journal. Instead I wrote about friendships. What feeds them and how do they fail? I wrote about college and the pressures that come along with so many expectations for excellence. I wrote about my eldest brother and how his attendance at Dartmouth College has pushed me towards Ivy League. I wrote about John, my boyfriend, who attends Roxbury Latin, a very prestigious, all boys, high school, just outside of Boston. I wrote about our relationship, and about next year, for he will be attending Stanford University. I wrote quite a bit on education in general. Sometimes I feel that it prohibits my success and that it limits who I am acquainted with. However, other times I can recall entries of gratitude towards my education at Oyster River.

Sometimes I pose a question and more often than not, I come to a conclusion that I am satisfied with and believe in. I have constant debates about life after death. Although I understand that God knows what I write in my journal, I feel it is the only place with which he cannot read. It sounds silly, yet my journal is a place I question my faith, bash religion and feed off of its imperfections. I am sure that I could fill an entire journal of questions I have proposed about my religion. It is a sour subject, for how uncomfortable I feel confiding in anyone other than my pages of such a personal relationship with a higher power.

As I am writing now, I feel strange, for I feel like I am a hermit or a psycho. I do converse with others regularly. I go out with friends, and I adore my family. Journaling just eats away a tiny piece of my time, a piece which others spend with aimless activities. I am a pretty good representation of a seventeen year old from New Hampshire. I just journal.

I hope my writing has given you some insight for your book. I enjoyed writing about this, if you couldn't tell. I have never really thought this in depth about my writing. I hope you can use some of this information to better your book, yet I know that "my type of journaling" differs from the scholastic reader-writer journals. I feel that my creative and reflective writing skills stemmed from my eighth grade year, the journals, and the activities you gave us. I also feel that you shared in me a confidence in my writing that allowed me to want to pursue it further. The Promising Young Writers of the Future, the constant feedback, and countless submissions for awards, planted a determination and fearlessness in my writing that still has not worn away.

Thanks again.

Lil

Monday, February 26 8:32 a.m.

Dear Lil,

I am so impressed with all you just wrote. You have truly made these journals so important to your being. Your big questions. Your wonderings. Even your way of describing what you do is poetic. "A page might smooth over a disagreement and propose an apology." "A phrase can erase an entire week of tension." Everything I ever hoped someone would make of them.

I am even thinking, if it is okay with you, that I would like to use this reply as the opening lead to the entire notion of Writer's-Reader's Notebooks. There will be a guide book for teachers, with lots of examples from many students' notebooks/journals in eighth grade, and an actual notebook or journal for kids to keep—published with my handouts and suggestions, the sections all set up, and passages from kids and authors about keeping journals.

I am curious that the journals have little about your reading. Why do you think that is? It makes me wonder if I should expect less about reading in kids' journals in 8th grade. To be honest, my journals have little about my reading also, so I wonder why that is?

Thanks so much for taking the time to write and explain how you use these to me. Sounds like you are doing as beautifully as I expected!

Take care—and if you have another minute, let me know what you think about little writing about reading. You continue to amaze me with your incredibly thoughtful and beautiful writing.

Mrs. Rief

Friday, March 02 5:42 p.m.

Subject: RE: JOURNALS!

Mrs. Rief,

I would be honored to have my letter part of your book! That is so exciting! Thank you so much! As for your question . . .

Unfortunately, reading is not considered a leisure activity for me anymore. I used to enjoy sitting down and being able to relax with a book. Now, I read in order to reach Chapter 23 of Jane Eyre because I have an in class essay the next morning. I read Bread Givers so I will be able to construct an essay due the following week. The amount I have to read for school is almost ridiculous. I am taking two classes which require a lot of reading, British Literature and American Studies. The writing that I do about the books that I read is in essay format and they are almost always assigned.

I am not sure if this applies to everyone and their journals, yet for a teenage girl who spends way too much time on homework, the last thing I want to write is a character analysis in my spare time. I love reading, yet with the pressures of school and other responsibilities I have no time to sit down with a good book. If I want to relax, I listen to music or sleep.

I feel that there are also many distractions which take away valuable reading time. The television, the Internet, and other electronic devices take away reading time. This answers the question of why do kids not read anymore. Not to talk about my boyfriend again, yet he is such a great example. He is brilliant and as a child he read. Instead of doing things that most children wanted to do, he hibernated in his room with books. I truly think that this is one of the stepping stones for his successes. I have been trying to instill this concept in my youngest sister, who is six.

I wish I read more. Reading other works can improve your own writing and especially your vocabulary. In some of my journal entries, I have made references to characters or events from books for comparison purposes. I just feel that the journal is a place for non scholastic writing. I am constantly surrounded by writing for school purposes, yet when I write for myself, I write about things that school does not cover.

I hope this helped. Happy snow day!

Lil

References and Recommended Resources

Allen, Janet. 1999. *Words, Words, Words: Teaching Vocabulary in Grades 4–12*. Portland, ME: Stenhouse.

Buckner, Aimee. 2005. *Notebook Know-How: Strategies for the Writer's Notebook*. Portland, ME: Stenhouse.

Carnicelli, Thomas. 2001. *Words Work: Activities for Developing Vocabulary, Style, and Critical Thinking*. Portsmouth, NH: Boynton/Cook.

Collins, Billy. 2001. *Sailing Alone Around the Room*. New York: Random House.

Ernst, Karen. 1997. *A Teacher's Sketch Journal: Observations on Learning and Teaching*. Portsmouth, NH: Heinemann.

Karen has taught me that sketching in my notebook is about paying attention, looking closely. She writes: "Remind yourself that you are keeping a journal not because you want to come up with things to do in your classroom but because you want to think, question, uncover new ideas. Take notes on what you read, quote your students, but make sure you include what you think these things mean" (9). Karen has taught me how to look closely at my students, pay attention to them, listen to them. When I draw them, I think about all I see, hear, wonder about each of them.

Feelings, Tom. 1993. *Soul Looks Back in Wonder*. New York: Dial.

Fletcher, Ralph. 1996a. *Breathing in, Breathing Out: Keeping a Writer's Notebook*. Portsmouth, NH: Heinemann.

This book made me realize all a notebook can be, inspiring me with lots of ideas and examples that are easily adapted or used as Ralph describes them with adolescents. If I had the resources, I would buy this book for each of my students to help them use their W-RN to the greatest advantage.

———. 1996b. *A Writer's Notebook: Unlocking the Writer Within You*. New York: Avon.

———. 1998. *Room Enough for Love*. New York: Aladdin.

Fulwiler, Toby, ed. 1987. *The Journal Book*. Portsmouth, NH: Boynton/Cook.

This book, along with Don Murray's daybook, influenced my thinking about journals and notebooks more than any other resource. It is the evidence of all journals can do. "In this book journals are seen in every situation and from every angle, as if mounted on a slow turntable under a spotlight. The conclusion of most of the students and teachers using them is that they get people thinking, they help them test their own experience against the ideas of many others. . . . As they become more and more engaged, they often write more clearly, and their journal entries display fewer mistakes. . . . They learn to think, not by doing exercises in a faddish 'critical thinking' textbook, but by working their way through real questions, with real interest and real intent" (from the Foreword, by Ken Macrorie).

Graham, Paula W. 1999. *Speaking of Journals: Children's Book Writers Talk About Their Diaries, Notebooks, and Sketchbooks.* Honesdale, PA: Caroline House.

Greenfield, Eloise. 1981. *Daydreamers.* New York: Dial.

Harwayne, Shelley. 1992. *Lasting Impressions: Weaving Literature into the Writing Workshop.* Portsmouth, NH: Heinemann.
Chapter 7, "Literature and the Writer's Notebook" (126–49), is filled with ways of launching and using notebooks with younger children, but all are easily adapted to older kids. A terrific resource.

Hubbard, Ruth Shagoury, and Karen Ernst, eds. 1996. *New Entries: Learning by Writing and Drawing.* Portsmouth, NH: Heinemann.

Janeczko, Paul. 1991. *Preposterous: Poems of Youth.* New York: Orchard.

Juster, Norton. 1961. *The Phantom Tollbooth.* New York: Yearling Books.

Knudson, R. R., and May Swenson. 1988. *American Sports Poems.* New York: Orchard.

MacGowan, Christopher, ed. 2004. *Poetry for Young People: William Carlos Williams.* New York: Sterling.

Murray, Donald M. 1990a. *Shoptalk: Learning to Write with Writers.* Portsmouth, NH: Boynton/Cook.

———. 1990b. *Write to Learn.* Fort Worth, TX: Holt, Rinehart and Winston.

National Conference Teachers of English (NCTE). 2007. *The Council Chronicle.* Urbana, IL.

Oliver, Mary. 1992. *New and Selected Poems.* Boston: Beacon.

Philbrick, Rodman. 1993. *Freak the Mighty.* New York: Scholastic.

Rief, Linda. 1992. *Seeking Diversity: Language Arts with Adolescents.* Portsmouth, NH: Heinemann.
Contains many examples of students' responses, reactions, and reflections on their reading and writing from their writer's-reader's logs in the appendix of portfolios, including ways to get them started writing in their logs (notebooks).

———. 2003. *100 Quickwrites.* New York: Scholastic.

———. 2003. *Voices from the Middle.* "A Reader's-Writer's Notebook: It's a Good Idea." Vol. 10 (4).

Romano, Tom. 1987. *Clearing the Way.* Portsmouth, NH: Heinemann.

Schmidt, Gary D., ed. 1994. *Poetry for Young People: Robert Frost.* New York: Sterling.

Sipe, Rebecca Bowers. 2003. *They Still Can't Spell? Understanding and Supporting Challenged Spellers in Middle and High School.* Portsmouth, NH: Heinemann.
  Beautifully written with many ways to reinforce for kids the reasons for caring about spelling, with examples that support all students.

Stafford, William. 1998. *The Way It Is: New and Selected Poems.* Minnesota: Graywolf.

Wilbur, Richard. 1998. *New and Collected Poems.* San Diego: Harcourt Brace Jovanovich.

Books Written as Diaries, Especially Relevant to Adolescents

Every one of the books listed here has either excerpts or whole pages that make great examples to show kids. Having a copy of a page from each picture book, or several passages from the books that are actual diary entries or talk about journals, helps kids see the many ways they could go about using their own *W-RN.*

Anonymous. 1998. *Go Ask Alice.* New York: Aladdin.

Boulton, Jane. 1984. *Opal: The Journal of an Understanding Heart.* New York: Crown.
  Opal Whitely lost her parents before she was five, was given to the wife of a lumberman, and lived in nineteen lumber camps in Oregon before she was twelve. A precocious child, she kept the scraps of her life in a diary, which a foster sister discovered and tore into fragments. After hearing bits of her life story at age twenty, an editor for Atlantic Monthly *asked if she had ever kept a diary. It took her nine months to piece it together, but the diary was published by Atlantic Monthly Press as* The Story of Opal. *This is a rearranged version, but the words are Opal's. A sad but touching story written in poetry form.*

Denenberg, Barry. 2000. *One Eye Laughing, the Other Weeping: The Diary of Julie Weiss.* New York: Scholastic.
  I have two shelves in my classroom filled with the Dear America books, all written in diary format. Although these are fictional accounts of real events and settings, they are well researched historically and eloquently written by writers such as Barry Denenberg, Kathryn Lasky, Patricia McKissack, Susan Bartoletti, Karen Hesse, Ann Turner, Ann Rinaldi, and Jim Murphy. This one focuses on a young girl in the Holocaust.

Frank, Anne. 1995. *The Diary of a Young Girl: Anne Frank.* New York: Doubleday.
  When I am teaching the Holocaust, I usually show the newest movie about Anne Frank's life or the movie The Attic, *from the perspective of Miep Gies, the courageous woman who hid the Frank*

family. As a way to introduce Anne and all she had to endure while in hiding, I copy twelve to fourteen entries from her diary and hand them out to the girls in the class before I begin the movie. At several appropriate junctures in the movie, some of which actually show Anne writing in her diary, I pause the film. I ask five to six girls to read their diary entry aloud. We continue the movie. At another spot, I pause the movie. Several more girls read. We do this about three times. They read the entries chronologically. Through the voices of today's fourteen-year-olds, we realize that Anne was just like them. We hear her/their voices. Once kids hear her voice, they want to read all she wrote. It is a compelling introduction to her diary.

After the reading of her diary entries, I ask all the students in the class to choose one (I have several copies of each of them prepared), glue it into their notebook, and write a response to all that Anne's words bring to mind for them.

Gantos, Jack. 1997. *Jack's Black Book*. New York: Farrar, Straus and Giroux.

———. 2002. *A Hole in My Life*. New York: Farrar, Straus and Giroux.

In both of these books by Jack Gantos, there are a number of references to how he uses and thinks about journals, either in his real life or as a fictional character. There are several excerpts worth reading aloud to kids, especially as an invitation to the whole book.

Gruwell, Erin. 1999. *The Freedom Writers Diary: How a Teacher and 150 Teens Used Writing to Change Themselves and the World Around Them*. New York: Doubleday.

Knight, Joan MacPhail. 2000. *Charlotte in Giverny*. San Francisco: Chronicle.

While living in France in 1892, Charlotte, a young (fictional) American girl, writes a journal of her experiences, including those among the Impressionist painters at the artist colony. Biographical sketches of the artists along with museum reproductions and watercolors enhance the intriguing journal entries.

Little, Jean. 1986. *Hey World, Here I Am!* Toronto: Kids Can.

Moss, Marissa. 1998. *Rachel's Journal: The Story of a Pioneer Girl*. Orlando, FL: Harcourt Brace.

This is a work of fiction but is based on the lives of many of the families who traveled the Oregon Trail from 1846 to 1868 as told through the diaries of women and children.

Townsend, Sue. 1982. *The Secret Diary of Adrian Mole, Age 13¾*. New York: Avon Books.

———. 1985. *The Growing Pains of Adrian Mole*. New York: Avon Books.

———. 1994. *Adrian Mole: The Lost Years*. New York: Soho Press.

Ulrich, Laurel Thatcher. 1990. *A Midwife's Tale: The Life of Martha Ballard, Based on Her Diary, 1785–1812*. New York: Vintage.

Ulrich won a Pulitzer Prize for this book. It is no wonder. She helps us understand so much of the society of the time through the steadfast words and actions of Martha Ballard and what they might mean. This is a truly intriguing book, but perhaps only for the most sophisticated adolescent readers.

Resources to Get Kids Started Writing in Their Notebooks

Bagdasarian, Adam. 2002. *First French Kiss*. New York: Farrar, Straus and Giroux.

Cisneros, Sandra. 1989. *The House on Mango Street*. New York: Vintage.

Gendler, J. Ruth. 1988. *The Book of Qualities*. New York: HarperPerenniel.

Harwayne, Shelley. 2005. *Novel Perspectives: Writing Minilessons Inspired by the Children in Adult Fiction*. Portsmouth, NH: Heinemann.

Heard, Georgia. 1995. *Writing Toward Home: Tales and Lessons to Find Your Way*. Portsmouth, NH: Heinemann.

———. 1999. *Awakening the Heart: Exploring Poetry in Elementary and Middle School*. Portsmouth, NH: Heinemann.

Lyon, George Ella. 1999. *Where I'm from, Where Poems Come From*. Spring, TX: Absey.

Rief, Linda. 2003. *100 Quickwrites: Fast and Effective Freewriting Exercises*. New York: Scholastic.

Scieszka, Jon. 2005. *Guys Write for Guys Read*. New York: Viking.

Sidman, Joyce. 2003. *The World According to Dog: Poems and Teen Voices*. Boston: Houghton Mifflin.

Resources Focused on Putting Books in Kids' Hands

Appleman, Deborah. 2006. *Reading for Themselves: How to Transform Adolescents into Lifelong Readers Through Out-of-Class Book Clubs*. Portsmouth, NH: Heinemann.

Atwell, Nancie. 1998. *In the Middle: New Understandings About Writing, Reading, and Learning*. Portsmouth, NH: Boynton/Cook.

———. 2007. *The Reading Zone: How to Help Kids Become Skilled, Passionate, Habitual, Critical Readers*. New York: Scholastic.

Blasingame, James. 2007. *Books That Don't Bore 'Em: Young Adult Books That Speak to This Generation*. New York: Scholastic.

Lesesne, Teri S. 2006. *Naked Reading: Uncovering What Tweens Need to Become Lifelong Readers*. Portland, ME: Stenhouse.

Using a Notebook as a Nature Journal and Sketchbook

These are not the only resources on nature journaling, but I have found they are the most helpful in offering the clearest and most useful techniques when working with students.

In using the three following books to teach simple drawing techniques, I often copy a sketch related to what we might be seeing (rocks, trees, flowers, etc.), make a copy for each of the students, and have them glue the sketch into their notebook and sketch or write down a technique the artist used to capture the object.

Arnosky, Jim. 1982. *Drawing from Nature*. New York: Lothrop, Lee and Shepard.

Leslie, Clare Walker, and Charles E. Roth. 2000. *Keeping a Nature Journal*. North Adams, MA: Storey.

Nice, Claudia. 2001. *How to Keep a Sketchbook Journal*. Cincinnati: North Light.

The next two books are the professional resources I return to again and again as the richest professional resources for the what, the why, and the how of nature or environmental studies through observation, sketching, reading, and writing. Both show how to begin with a journal or notebook and show how to take these observations and initial ideas to more polished products of persuasion, narration, and exposition of art and writing.

Chancer, Joni, and Gina Rester-Zodrow. 1997. *Moon Journals: Writing, Art, and Inquiry Through Focused Nature Study*. Portsmouth, NH: Heinemann.

Rous, Emma. 2000. *Literature and the Land: Reading and Writing for Environmental Literacy, 7–12.* Portsmouth, NH: Boynton/Cook.

Books About People Who Kept Nature Journals and What They Learned

Armstrong, Jennifer. 2003. *Audubon, Painter of Birds in the Wild Frontier*. New York: Harry N. Abrams.
Armstrong used Audubon's own journals as her primary resource for this book.

Arnosky, Jim. 1983. *Secrets of a Wildlife Watcher*. New York: Lothrop, Lee and Shepard.
From Arnosky's journal notes and sketches, we learn his techniques for finding and getting close enough to observe their behavior.

———. 2005. *Hook, Line, and Sinker: A Beginner's Guide to Fishing, Boating, and Watching Water Wildlife*. New York: Scholastic.
Filled with the drawings from his fishing journals, this book also has photographs that enhance all

Arnosky has to teach about watching water wildlife. A beautiful book that shows kids another way to use their notebooks to observe in the outdoors.

Burleigh, Robert. 2003. *Into the Woods: John James Audubon Lives His Dream*. New York: Atheneum.

From the author's note: "Audubon was a famous early American woodsman and artist.... This story, illustrated with beautiful paintings by Wendell Minor, consists of an imaginary letter in which Audubon explains to his father why he has chosen the unique life he leads.... Quotations, taken from Audubon's journals, further emphasize the profound world view of this remarkable man."

Carroll, David M. 2001. *Swampwalker's Journal: A Wetland's Year*. New York: Houghton-Mifflin.

Carroll's words and sketches put us in the wetlands, allowing us to realize how closely we need to look if we really want to understand the value of saving these areas and the creatures that live there.

——. 2004. *Portrait with Turtles: A Memoir*. New York: Houghton-Mifflin.

Crocitto, Frank, ed. 2000. *New Suns Will Arise: From the Journals of Henry David Thoreau*. New York: Hyperion.

This book is a combination of selected journal entries with the photography of John Dugdale, capturing the strength and spirit of Thoreau.

Duncan, Dayton, and Ken Burns. 1997. *Lewis and Clark: An Illustrated History*. New York: Alfred A. Knopf.

This is the companion volume to the PBS television series on Lewis and Clark and contains extensive excerpts from the journals kept by the captains and the enlisted men, as well as a wealth of diary sketches.

Krupinski, Loretta. 1992. *Celia's Island Journal*. Boston: Little, Brown.

This is an adaptation of Celia Thaxter's Among the Isles of Shoals. *Through journal entries, the author tells the story of Celia as a young girl, growing up in the mid-nineteenth century on an isolated island off the coast of New Hampshire, where her father is the keeper of the lighthouse.*

Pettenati, Jeanne K. 2006. *Galileo's Journal 1609–1610*. Watertown, MA: Charlesbridge.

This fictional journal, which contains actual biographical information, is from the year in which Galileo constructed his own telescope and began to record his astronomical discoveries.

Roth, Susan. 1990. *Marco Polo: His Notebook*. New York: Doubleday.

Although this is a fictional account of Marco Polo's travels, it uses authentic-sounding diary entries along with illustrations of actual prints, photographs, and maps.

Schmidt, Thomas, and Jeremy Schmidt. 1999. *The Saga of Lewis and Clark into the Uncharted West*. New York: DK.

This book is equally as appealing as the Duncan and Burns book, with photographs, actual diary excerpts, eloquent writing, and vast amounts of compelling information.

Sis, Peter. 1998. *Tibet Through the Red Box*. New York: Scholastic.

Opening the red box, Sis finds the diary his father kept when he was lost in Tibet in the mid-1950s. This is as much the return of a father to his son as it is a journey into Tibet.

———. 2003. *The Tree of Life: A Book Depicting the Life of Charles Darwin, Naturalist, Geologist, Thinker.* New York: Farrar, Straus and Giroux.

Presents the life of the famous nineteenth-century naturalist using text from Darwin's writings and detailed drawings by Sis.

Webb, Sophie. 2003. *My Season with Penguins: An Antarctic Journal.* Boston: Houghton Mifflin.

Describes Webb's two-month stay in Antarctica through her journals and drawings to tell the story of penguins.

Wright-Frierson, Virginia. 1996. *A Desert Scrapbook: Dawn to Dusk in the Sonoran Desert.* New York: Simon and Schuster.

Using journal entries, sketches, and paintings, Wright-Frierson introduces us to the plants and animals of the Sonoran Desert.

———. 1999. *A North American Rain Forest Scrapbook.* New York: Walker.

Using journal entries, sketches, and paintings, Wright-Frierson describes the plants and animals she found by exploring North America's only rain forest, in Washington State.

Appendix: Classroom Examples

1. Sarah's Picture Name

2. Mrs. Rief's Sample Reading List

3. Dan's and Kaitlin's Sample Reading Lists
   What do you notice about each list? What could you say about Dan as a reader? About Kaitlin as a reader?

4. Eighth-Grade Language Arts Curriculum Overview

5. Notes for the Teacher to Guide Students' Notebook Response

6. Two Quickwrite Activities

7. Bookmark

8. Writing-Reading Survey

9. Samples from the "Notes" Section of Students' Notebooks
   a. Sample from Amy's Notes over a Two-Week Period
   b. Exercise to show kids how to respond to other students' writing. One person had to put a wad of paper in a bag while standing with his/her back to the bag. Classmates were told they could help the person with verbal comments. (Adapted from a young teacher in Minnesota with thanks.)
      ◆ Marcela's Notes: Responding to Writers
      ◆ Robbie's Notes: Responding to Writers
      ◆ Compiled Notes Comparing Responding to Paper Bag Toss with Responding to Writing
   c. Emiliano's Notes on Storyboards and on the Language of Cartoons

10. Vocabulary
    Example in Written Format
    Example in Chart Format
    Example in Drawn Format
    Specialized Vocabulary with Vignettes to Illustrate
    Content-Area Vocabulary: *Inertia; Radiant Energy*

Sarah's Picture Name

Mrs. Rief's Sample Reading List

Reading List: Books I Am Currently Reading

Title	# of pages	Author	Date Begun	Date Finished	Degree of Difficulty: Easy / Just Right / Hard	Rating 1 2 3 4 5	Best one word description
Stones from the River		Hegi	summer	Sept.	hard	4+	complex characters
What Jamie Saw		Coman			E	4	lead
When Elephants Weep			Sept. 13		H		abandoned - too didactic
The Sixteen Pleasures		Hellenga	Oct. 11	Oct. 11	A	4	
The Barn		Avi	Nov. 4	Nov. 8	E very	3	Made me think of mom! and "I could write that!"
The English Patient		Ondaatje				5+	Beautiful language - complex story
Tunes for Bears to Dance To		Cormier				4	Holocaust
Dear Anne Frank - poems		Angosin				2	She sounds angry. Only 2-3 poems I liked.
The Peaceable Classrm.		O'Reilly				5+	I must write to her.
Two Old Women		Wallis	July 30	July 31	E	4	Heartwarming story.
Never in a Hurry		N.S. Nye	Sept.	Oct. 3	A	5	So many wonderful stories.
Out of the Dust		Hesse	Oct. 17	Oct. 17	E	4+	Read aloud - novel in poetry.
You Gotta Be the Book		Wilhelm	Nov.	Apr.	A	4+	teacher - researcher - opening books to kids -
Ellen Foster		Gibbons				5	
Cold Mountain		Frazier	Feb.			5	Read slowly - didn't want this to end
A Cure for Dreams		Gibbons	Apr. 16	Apr. 17	E	3+	Read on plane - Hard time remembering story!
True North		Lasky	Aug.	Aug.	E	4+	young girl - slave - Boston wonderful -
California Blue		Klass	"	"	E	4+	admirable charac. moral dilemma
Memoirs of a Geisha		Golden	Aug.	Dec.	A	5	
Rules of the Road		Bauer	Sept.	Oct.	E		
Soldier's Heart		Paulsen	90 min.		E	4	
The Reader		Schlenk	Nov.	Dec.	A		A total surprise! Provocative! Don't know what to think.
Evening		Minot	Jan.	Feb.	A		Sad - is it ok to have loved once yet never again? Hard to read - mom - cancer -
The Schernoff Discoveries		Paulsen	Mar.		EEE		
Mosaic of Thought		Keene-Z.	July			4.+	So much to think about - use
On the Beach		Shute			E-A	4	Finally understood as adult - how do kids relate to this - ? -

Dan's and Kaitlin's Sample Reading Lists

Dan's

Reading List: Books I Am Currently Reading

Title	# of pages	Author	Date Begun	Date Finished	Degree of Difficulty Easy Just Right Hard	Rating 1 2 3 4 5 Best one word description
Swift Rivers	270	C. Meigs	9/14	9/30	E/JR	descriptive 4
Sacred Clowns Oops!		T. Hillerman	10/7	11/14	JR	boring 3
Sphere	371	M. Crichton	11/15	12/3	JR	good ending 4
Harris and Me		G. Paulsen	11/29	11/30	JR	good 5
The Crossing		G.P.	11/30	12/1	JR	good 3
The River		G.P.	12/1	12/2	JR	good 4
Tiltawhirl John		G.P.	12/2	12/5	JR	NOT SO GOOD
Father Water, Mother Woods		G.P.	12/2		JR	very relaxed 4
Deerslayer	541	J.F. Cooper	1/9		H	
Juniper	198	M. Furlong	1/25	1/31	JR	fast reading 4
Wise Child	228	"	2/1	2/4	JR	just as fast reading 4
Muke Lemonade		V.E. Wolff	3/3	3/10	JR	interesting read 4
Monkey Island		P. Fox	3/23		JR	
The Giver	180	L. Lowry	4/?	4/11	JR	good 4

Kaitlin's

Reading List: Books I Am Currently Reading

Title	# of pages	Author	Date Begun	Date Finished	Degree of Difficulty Easy Just Right Hard	Rating 1 2 3 4 5 Best one word description
Dragonflight		McCaffrey	2/1	2/3	JR	5+ triumphant
Crystal Singer		"	2/3	2/4	JR	5 romantic
Letters from Rifka		Hesse	2/5	2/5	E	4 hopeful
Night		Wiesel	2/6	2/10	E	5+ numbing
2001 A Space Odyssey		Clarke	2/8	2/17	JR/H	5 captivating
The Rowan		McCaffrey	2/15	2/16	E	5+ fascinating
Field Guide to the Night Sky	400		2/14	2/16	H	5 informative
The Lost Mind		Pike	2/18	2/19	E	4 gruesome
Killashandra		McCaffrey	2/20	2/20	JR	5 romantic
Night-again		Wiesel	2/26	2/26	E	5+ numbing
Ender's Game		Card	2/26	2/26	JR	5+ exhilerating
Friedrich		Richter				
Number the Stars		Lowry				

Eighth-Grade Language Arts Curriculum Overview

(Note: This may change from year to year.)

I expect the eighth-grade students to

- read for a half hour each night (reading of their choice—fiction or nonfiction)
- collect/respond/react/reflect daily in/to/on their writing and reading in their *W-RN* (one to three pages per week)
- maintain a list of books they are currently reading
- maintain the "Notes" section in the *W-RN* for all lessons from class
- find and define two to four vocabulary words per week in the "Vocabulary" section of the *W-RN*
- take two pieces of writing to final draft every four weeks (maintenance of portfolio)
- set quarterly goals
- evaluate themselves as learners each quarter

Within this framework of expectations, I use different themes and ideas for teaching various kinds of writing and reading. The students have choice within this framework. They read on their own, we read literature together, and I often read out loud to them. Students often choose what they want to write and in what format. There are other times when I ask them to try certain kinds of writing and reading. The students are the final decision makers about what works or what doesn't work for them—what gets graded and what doesn't.

I care deeply about the process students go through as they read and write and about the products they craft. I want them to learn how to learn, but I also want them to become the strongest writers and readers possible within the time constraints we have. I expect, teach, and guide students in the rethinking of their writing and the editing of pieces using the appropriate grammatical constructions and conventions (including usage, spelling, punctuation, capitalization, agreement, etc.).

In eighth grade my general theme for the year is *choices*, and I give them the following overview of the focus for each quarter.

Quarter 1

This is an introduction to, and immersion in, writing and reading through students' own choices, guided by the following questions: Who are you? What are the choices you make as a writer and reader? When given options, what are the choices you make as a person?

- free verse poetry, letter about literature, personal narrative or memoir, reading response, writing of choice, self-evaluations, storyboarding or drawing as thinking

◆ books of choice to read individually, ones I may read to you (*Love That Dog,* by Sharon Creech), and whole-class reading of same book (*Freak the Mighty,* by Rodman Philbrick, or *The Outsiders,* by S. E. Hinton)

Quarter 2

Who are the authors you admire most? What are the choices they make as they craft writing? How could the choices you notice they make in their writing influence and inform your writing and reading?

Students choose an author they admire to read and look at in depth based on the kind of writing they want to do better: fiction, nonfiction, poetry. (In groups of two or three, they choose an author whom they admire as a mentor to their writing. What can they learn as writers from the author's writing that they can try in their writing?)

Students will be writing a range of several pieces based on their choice of mentor author, including book reviews.

As a whole class we will be reading a novel such as *The Outsiders.*

Quarter 3: Exhibeo Humanitas

What happens when people's choices are limited? Or they have no choices at all? What are the consequences of those choices and/or lack of choices? What motivates human beings to make particular choices?

Students will read and write in response to whole-class and small-group reading and discussion of common books and individual choices, such as *Night* (Elie Wiesel), *Witness* (Karen Hesse), *Daniel's Story* (Carol Matas), *The Swallows of Kabul* (Yasmina Khadra), *The Book Thief* (Markus Zusak), *Sounder* (William Armstrong), *Shabanu* (Suzanne Staples), *Roots* (Alex Haley), *The Cage* (Ruth Minsky Sender), *Two Old Women (Velma Wallis), One Child* (Torey Hayden), *The Education of Little Tree* (Forrest Carter), *The Devil's Arithmetic* (Jane Yolen), *I Know Why the Caged Bird Sings* (Maya Angelou), *The Acorn People* (Ron Jones), *Lyddie* (Katherine Paterson), *The Drowning of Stephen Jones* (Bette Greene), *My Sister's Keeper* (Jodi Picoult), *In My Hands* (Irene Gut Opdyke).

As a whole class we will read and act out either the play version of *Anne Frank* or the shortened version of *Flowers for Algernon* (Daniel Keyes). We'll read *The Giver* (Lois Lowry) as a whole class and view several movies focused on the Holocaust.

Quarter 4: Writer's-Reader's Personal Research Project

Development of showcase portfolio, with a particular focus on writing and reading of choice. Through your choices all year, what have you done well that you would like to develop more fully, what would you like to do differently, or what would you like to do that you haven't attempted at all? How do your choices affect who you are as a reader, a writer, a person?

As a whole class we will read, act out, and view *Romeo and Juliet*. What are the consequences of the choices these young people and adults make? This will include reading, note taking, and interpreting specific scenes, and viewing, comparing, and contrasting scenes from film, live theatre, and plays.

Throughout the year students will be immersed in reading and writing of all genres: nonfiction, realistic fiction, historical fiction, young adult literature, short stories, poetry, graphic novels, essays, plays, biographies, children's literature, and picture books. Films, videos, guest experts, and field trips are meant to enhance the learning experience.

Notes for the Teacher to Guide Students' Notebook Response

Writing: We learn to write by writing. Your notebook is a place to play with ideas and words. It is a place to write your initial ideas.

Books: You choose your own books or magazine articles. Try to be reading a book at all times. If you don't like it, abandon it and find another.

Reading: We learn to read, and to write, by reading. I expect you to read for a half hour each night, ___ nights per week. Friday is silent reading day in class. We will read some things together. Others will be read to us or by us.

Your written response does not always have to be about the book you are reading. What you write or draw in your *W-RN* should be what you want to preserve or remember about your thinking and living. Written and illustrated pages are your thoughts about, reactions to, interpretations of, and questions about what you are reading, writing, observing, thinking in and about the world around you. Your comments may be in response to the author's process as a writer or your process as a reader, writer, and learner. If you are stuck, you might try one of the following:

- *Quote or point out a particular line or passage*. Write about facts or lines that you hear or read that surprise you, fascinate you, anger you, and so on. Quote a part of the book, your own writing, or something you hear or read that you think is an example of good writing. What do you like about the passage? What makes this good writing? Why do you want to save it?

- *Jot down experiences or memories*. How does this reading make you think or feel? What does it bring to mind? What kinds of ideas does this reading give you for writing?

- *React*. What reactions do you have to the world around you, other things you have read, learned, or discovered? Do you love/hate/can't stop reading this book? What makes you feel this way?

- *Question*. What confuses you? What don't you understand? Why did the author do something a particular way? What would you have done differently? What questions do you have about your own writing? About things you notice around you?

- *Evaluate*. How's your life going? How is your writing going? How's your world, the world at large doing? How does this book compare with others you have read? What makes it good or not so good?

- *Write your understanding*. What are the ideas or understandings you are taking from the book? What do you think is the "so what," or the reason it was written?

- *Collect.* Insert poems, song lyrics, pictures, photos, surveys, news articles, sayings that have to do with who you are/anything you want to remember as a writer, reader, thinker, listener, participant, observer of the world around you.

Receiving Response to Your Writer's-Reader's Notebook

During the year you will be looking back on and using your responses, records, and reactions to your reading and writing to see how you have grown and changed. You will share your notebook with me, peers of your choice, and sometimes parents. Our response to you is meant to "affirm what you know, challenge your thinking, and extend your learning" (Atwell 1998).

Two Quickwrite Activities (from Rief 2003)

Crossing the River

Sitting with me
On a hillside
Looking down and across
A green valley,
My father
Once said to me
You never step
Into the same river twice.

I nodded
Like I understood
What he said.
That was then.
When I step
Onto a soccer field
Or out the door to school
Or open any book
Now
Now I know what he meant.

—*Jesse S.*

Try this:

◆ Write as quickly as you can, for two to three minutes, all that this poem brings to mind for you.

◆ Borrow any line and write off or from that line as quickly and as specifically as you can, letting the line lead your thinking.

◆ Thinking of the line "You never step into the same river twice," write as quickly as you can all that comes to mind for you.

When I Was Young at the Ocean

With thanks to Cynthia Rylant for When I Was Young in the Mountains

When I was young at the ocean, I sat at the edge of the wooden pier and dangled my toes in the water. Like tiny rowboats my toes skimmed the rolling waves, ever alert for sharks. Sometimes I sat cross-legged in shorts and tee-shirt, a bamboo fishing pole stretched to catch mackerel. No one ever told me to bait the hook.

When I was young at the ocean, I cracked open mussels and periwinkles and clams, and ran my fingers across their gushy insides. I squished seaweed nodules between my forefinger and thumb, anxious for the pop and spray from the moist insides.

When I was young at the ocean, I burned my shoulders and smelled of Noxzema through the entire month of July. I drank in the aroma of hip roses, salt water, and seaweed. At low tide I played croquet with the Queen of Hearts, flew to the moon in a hammock, and fed my dolls deviled ham sandwiches in the shade of the screened house.

As the tide came in, water lapped at the rocky shore. The skin of my feet toughened as I paced those rounded stones, my eyes searching for skippers. *When I was young, I never wished to climb the mountains, or live in the city, or camp in the forest. The ocean was enough. It still is.*

—Linda Rief

Try this:

- Think of a place that you love being (mountains, sitting in an oak tree, a fort, lake, etc.) and as quickly as you can in two to three minutes, write down all you see, smell, touch, hear, taste, and do there.

- Borrow Rylant's line "When I was young in the" or "at the" and write as quickly as you can all that comes to mind about that place.

Bookmark

"Read like a wolf eats."
—Gary Paulsen

As you read, consider the following* when you write or sketch in your journal:

I wonder about . . .
I'm surprised by . . .
I like how . . .
. . . reminded me . . .
I don't see . . .
Maybe . . .
The author . . .
I wish . . .
I understand . . .
I can't understand . . .
I love the way . . .
I noticed . . .
Why did . . .
I feel . . .
I imagine . . .
I think . . .
I realized . . .
I believe . . .
If I were . . .
I was confused by . . .

Note the following:
Questions that come to mind.
What motivates characters?
Surprises in wording!
Compelling leads! Endings!
Passages that seem to say, "This is the
    significance of this writing."

Respond deeply.
Write honestly.
Admit confusion.
Discover and expand on the author's ideas.
Attempt to discover your own ideas about
    writing, about reading, about books,
    about yourself.

Writing-Reading Survey

(adapted from Atwell's *In the Middle* [1998])

Please answer the following questions in the "Notes" section of your *Writer's-Reader's Notebook*. Answer as thoroughly as possible. Date your response. Refer to specific pieces of writing you have done or specific things you have read as you answer each question.

1. What does someone have to do in order to be a good writer? How do you know that?

2. What is the easiest part of writing for you? (What do you do well?)

3. What is the hardest part of writing for you?

4. How do you come up with ideas for writing?

5. What is the best piece of writing you've ever done? What made it so good?

6. What helps you the most to make your writing better?

7. Why is it important to be able to write well?

8. What happens to your finished pieces of writing?

9. What does someone have to do in order to be a good reader? How do you know that?

10. What are all the different kinds of reading you do (in school and out of school)? Not just books—anything.

11. What kind of reading is the easiest for you to understand? What makes it easy?

12. What makes reading difficult for you? How do you overcome those difficulties? (When you don't understand something you've read, what do you do to make sense of it?)

13. How do you go about finding and choosing books or other writing to read?

14. What's the best book you ever read? (List one to three books.) What made it (them) so good?

15. Why is it important to know how to read well?

16. What are your goals as a writer for the next eight weeks? (What expectations do you have for yourself?) How can I help you meet those goals?

17. What are your goals as a reader for the next eight weeks? (What expectations do you have for yourself?) How can I help you meet those goals?

18. Is there anything else you would like me to know about you as a reader or writer that these questions haven't let you tell me?

Sample from Amy's Notes
over several weeks

9/12   ellipsis = 3 periods
        more words to come
        words that are missing

9/18   quotation marks - if it's the same person talking, you
put quotations only at the beginning of each paragraph
and then at the very end
- also use quotation marks for the title of a poem or the
title of a short story
underlining - titles of complete works

10/25   Effective Writing
good description - imagls
setting   through sense of taste, touch, smell, hearing, sight
character
new and interesting vocab./language
phrasing in unique or unexpected ways
vivid - in ability to make it realistic
right amount of description
writer + reader believe story
voice
identify with character
*point to writing - think, feel, learn
tension - holds off reader, pulls reader in
use of similes, metaphor - naturally
complications on way to resolution of problem
reader feels present
conventions of language - handwriting, sp., punctuation,
grammar - appropriate to piece
strong lead
strong ending
    I have learned a lot from constructing

this list of what makes a piece of effective
writing. One of the most important characteristics,
in my mind, is for the reader to think, feel, learn
something. Strong leads are also very important, as
well as strong endings.

10/26 interview: questions yes/no ≠ not helpful
(conference)   good questions elicit response
- focus on one thing that really interests you
lead

<u>Revising</u>

pointing out ⟶ ✓✓✓ (keeping?)
questions ⟶ (considering/weighing answers)
What if...? (phrase suggestions this way)

lead
                                    ↱ conditional, slows piece down
tense - time → simple present, past (could, would)
                                     (have, had)

should of have
should 've⸝
active voice
nouns - verbs (strongest)
  (seem, get, got) ← get rid of these words
details - sight, sound, taste, smell, touch
characters - ones we care about
"The bigger the issue, the smaller the detail."

©2007 by Linda Rief from *Inside the Writer's-Reader's Notebook*. Portsmouth, NH: Heinemann.

Samples from the "Notes" Section of Students' Notebooks

Sample from Amy's Notes over a Two-Week Period

Marcela's Notes: Responding to Writers

Robbie's Notes: Responding to Writers

Compiled Notes Comparing Responding to Paper Bag Toss with Responding to Writing

In Notes Section of WR Notebook draw stick figure and Key words - words that helped/didn't help person put wad of paper in bag.

Arc it- a little higher.

Move back a little

Throw to left

A little higher!

Way to go!

Keep trying!

Throw toward the sound of my voice.

Close!

Yeah! Good job!

Straighten your wrist!

Release earlier

Throw lighter.

What helped person get wad in bag?
Cheered her on/told what she did well
gave guidance - specific, exact
things to do
if close, suggested try it again
bad comments no help
That needs work!
Lousy shot! Terrible! You lose!
Thrower asking questions helps:
How close am I?
Higher? Lower?

In what ways is this connected to the way you respond to someone's writing
- need lots of drafts to hit mark
- feedback: constructive
specific
direct, not evasive
- take a risk- try something you might not usually do
- use other resources-people, books to perfect writing
- know not everything works

Emiliano's Notes on Storyboards and on the Language of Cartoons

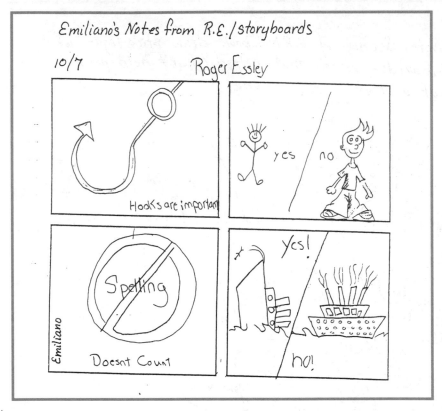

Vocabulary

Example in Written Format

EXAMPLE:
"In preparation for the project, student architects
built elaborate models of houses, gates, and buildings;
... even called a town meeting to <u>assuage</u> (e-swaj)
one <u>disgruntled</u> <u>abutter</u>."
> "When learning is 'out of control'"
> <u>The Boston Sunday Globe</u>
> Sept. 14

assuage: 1. to make less burdensome or painful; ease
2. to satisfy or appease, as thirst
★ 3. to pacify or calm

(Lat. ad + suavis to sweeten)

disgruntled: discontented, annoyed

abutter: to border on; be next to (refers to person)

Example in Chart Format

Date	Word (+ Origin)	Sentence	Book/Source	Definition
3/5	deluge	"I came out during the deluge."	My mom said it.	a drenching rain; in abundance
3/5	condescension	"The phouka smiled and inclined his head in lordly condescension."	War for the Oaks	2. patronizing attitude or behavior
3/6	enigmatic	"The dark glasses were wonderfully enigmatic."	War for the Oaks	mysterious + obscure
3/7	voraciously	"...but consume gasoline voraciously and belch clouds of exhaust."	New York Times article about a new insurance policy for SUVs	desiring or consuming in great quantities
3/8	fastidious	"Is Mr. Rochester an exacting, fastidious sort of man?"	Jane Eyre p. 103	attentive to detail and hard to please

Example in Drawn Format

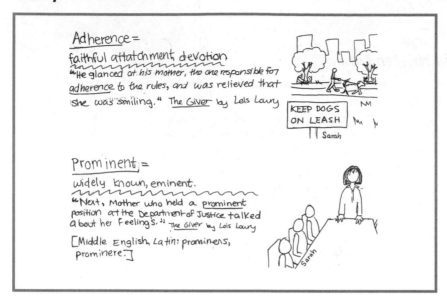

Content-Area Vocabulary: Inertia

Specialized Vocabulary with Vignettes to Illustrate

discrimination- To make distinctions on the basis of class or category without regard to individ-ual merit.   *regard*

examples:

When I went to soccer practice a while ago, we (my team) were going to have a practice session with the U=14 (under 14) boys. As the two teams were split, I heard one boy mutter to the other, "what a great team we have! All the other players are girls!" They descriminated against us because we're girls!

stereotyping- A conventional, formulaic, and oversimplified consep-tion, opinion, or image.   *opinion*

examples:

At the begining of my 6th grade year, my class had a very odd student. He had a million errings and gross cloths. I had seen bad people who looked like him on T.V, and just   *begin-beginning* *earrings* *clothes*

because I had, I was afraid of him. Later, I ended up really injoying talking to him, and my mind changed.   *enjoy*

---

intolerance- Unwilling to tollerate differences in opinions or beliefs.   *tolerate*

examples:

My neighbor accross the street practices a form of wit. raft. My dad believes in the Darwin theory. Whenever we talk about my neigh-bor, my dad bas no tollerance for her beliefs at all! His mind gets clouded so he isn't open to new ideas, which I think is too bad.   *across* *tolerance*

prejudice- An adverse judgment or opinion formed beforehand or without knowledge or examination of the facts.

examples:

When I went to overnight camp a year ago, there was a girl named Bethanie in my cabin. She had a skin deformity. When I had to pick a bunk, I didn't choose the one under her, because she was different. Later, I got to know her better, and she became areally great friend!

Kaitlin, terrific vignettes that illustrate each word so well. ← add to list please. (Just wanted to remind you about the spelling of the words in the margin 😊!)